The Captain & Me

On and Off the Field with Thurman Munson

♦

Ron Blomberg

with Dan Epstein

TRIUMPH
B O O K S

Library of Congress Cataloging-in-Publication Data available upon request.

This book is available in quantity at special discounts for your group or organization. For further information, contact:

Triumph Books LLC
814 North Franklin
Street Chicago, Illinois
60610 (312) 337-0747
www.triumphbooks.com

Printed in U.S.A.

ISBN: 978-1-63727-005-9

Design by Sue Knopf

For Beth—my love and inspiration.
—Ron

For Katie—with thanks for all the love,
belief, and support.
—Dan

Contents

Foreword

When Thurman and Ron first met, over 50 years ago, the Yankees were not in great shape. But they were the young up-and-comers, part of the hope for the team's future.

The team really felt like a family then. All of the guys were young and hungry, and all in the same boat—striving hard to be a good team, united in their quest to go forward and bring winning baseball back to the Bronx. None of them were superstars yet, but you had older players like Mel Stottlemyre and Jake Gibbs taking the younger guys under their wing, showing them and teaching them how to be major leaguers. There was such a nice feeling of camaraderie and brotherhood during that rebuilding process, and us wives were all lucky enough to be part of it. You never forget the beginnings; you just never do.

Thurman and Ron were buddies, no doubt about it. As everyone knows, Thurman was an intense competitor; to earn his respect as a player, you had to really show him that you would do anything to win. I think his bond with Ron just naturally grew out of the respect they had for each other as players, and the little-boy love of the game that they recognized in each other. Ron's little-boy heart was recognizable to anyone who ever met him; he was so unguarded and positive and upbeat, and the kind of exuberance and excitement he had about playing baseball is something you definitely want to see from someone on your team. Thurman had this tough and grumpy façade, so it was hard to see that little boy in him—I saw it because we were together from when I was 10 and he was 12, so I knew about the little boy that lived inside him. And Ron saw it, too.

Thurman trusted very few people; but if he felt safe with you, then he'd feel freer to be himself and to let that guard down. His childhood was not ideal; it scarred him, and there's no doubt in my mind that a lot of his bruises came to the surface as he got older. And Ron is one of those people who is sensitive to other people and their shortcomings and their hurts. So their relationship worked very well for Thurman, because he could have his unguarded moments with Ron where he didn't feel like he was being judged or compared to someone else.

Sportswriters got on Thurman right from the start because he wasn't a "yes man"—he wasn't the kind of guy who would give you the answer that you perhaps were looking for. How he saw things is how he would say it, and that rubbed people the wrong way a lot of times, whereas Ron would always find a way to charm whoever he was talking to. Thurman would tease him about that sometimes—he teased Ron all the time about all kinds of things, in a brotherly way—but I think he appreciated that Ron kept the sportswriters away from him, and he also kind of marveled at the fact that Ron could be this kind of charismatic character who could talk to anyone about anything. Neither of them were ever ashamed to be themselves; they definitely had that in common. But I think part of Thurman wished he could have been a little more like Ron.

Thurman had absolute respect for Ron as a person. In 1971, their first season together on the Yankees, Ron sat out the last couple of games of the year to be with his wife on Rosh Hashanah. And I remember Thurman having so much respect and admiration for that; it touched Thurman that Ron was that kind of deep-feeling person, and that he had the integrity to be able to say, "I choose not to play." That impressed Thurman greatly.

Thurman loved the baseball side of Ron, but he also loved the human side of him. And he felt so terrible for Ron when one injury after another was happening to him. He would tell me, "This guy cannot catch a break." Ron was someone who was so ready and so willing to be part of this great new chapter in Yankees history, and he wound up missing out on all of it. Thurman knew it could have been the same story for him, or for any of the other guys on the team at any given time, and he knew what it had to be doing to Ron's psyche. Thurman was a sensitive man, and he understood what Ron was going through, the pain that he was feeling.

Someone once called Thurman an "enigma," and it was so true; you could never really figure him out. I've met some fantastic people through my lifetime, Hollywood stars and politicians and so many people in so many different fields, and there's still never been a more interesting person to me than Thurman Munson, not ever. There were so many layers to him, and he kept a lot of things buried because he was so vulnerable. He would tell me that he didn't care if people knew or understood him, but I think it's such a shame that so many people missed the heart of that man. He had a tough skin, but I'm here to tell you that he was the singularly most tender man I've ever known.

So many of Thurman's teammates have opened up to me over the years about the Thurman they played with, and I've been so privileged to hear their stories; to this day, these guys are still so in love with Thurman and everything that he was, and everything that he brought to them and to the team. They got to see sides of him so few other people did, and see how phenomenal a person he was.

I was pleased to learn that Ron was writing a book about his friendship with Thurman, because I knew that he would treat Thurman fairly, and show a softer side of him that so many were not privy to. Of course, if Thurman were still here with us, he would say he didn't care about that kind of thing. But in addition to being a great ballplayer, he was a treasure—and speaking as the person who perhaps knew him better than anyone, I'm glad Ron is sharing that treasure with the world.

—Diana Munson
September 2020

Introduction

Thurman Munson hit a home run in the very first major league ballgame I ever attended. It was May 30, 1976, at Tiger Stadium, and Thurman's deep fly to the venerable ballpark's empty left-field upper deck capped the New York Yankees' 4–0 victory over my beloved Detroit Tigers.

I was 10 years old at the time, and the baseball bug had only bitten me about a month earlier, but I already knew who Thurman Munson was, well before my dad and I headed to "The Corner" together. Thanks to his 1976 Topps card (which pictured him wearing a thick beard, rumpled pinstripes, and a more-than-slightly irritated expression), I'd learned that this euphoniously-named dude was an All-Star catcher, and I'd read enough *Detroit Free Press* sports pages that spring to understand that he was one of the big reasons that the Yankees were off to such a hot start in 1976.

So while I should have been annoyed that Thurman had helped beat my team that warm Sunday afternoon, I was, in actuality, really thrilled to have seen him in action. My dad had scored us some sweet field-level seats behind home plate, which gave us an outstanding view of Thurman as he called the game, kibbitzed with Tigers hitters, occasionally went to the mound for a quick conference with Yankees hurler Rudy May, and generally took control of the diamond like he owned it. I knew I was watching one of the greats, and immediately decided—even though I wasn't a Yankees fan—to anoint Thurman as my favorite catcher.

I clearly wasn't alone in that regard. While Yankees fans understandably worship him to this day, I've met so many baseball aficionados over the years who loved Thurman Munson *despite* his association with the Yankees—people who deeply admired his abilities, his toughness, his dedication, his leadership, his salty sense of humor, his down-to-earth attitude, and his tendency to come through in the clutch, even though he often employed those very same qualities and characteristics in beating their favorite teams. We all still vividly remember where we were when we heard the news about his fatal plane crash in August 1979, of course: Me, I was staying at my grandparents' house in Freeport, Long Island, and I locked myself in their bathroom so that they couldn't see me crying. The murder of Angels outfielder Lyman Bostock the previous fall had been tragic and senseless and disturbing, but this one really felt like the loss of a family member.

There was another Yankees card that I pulled from my Topps packs in the spring of 1976, one of a guy named Ron Blomberg. I had no idea who he was, but my dad had taught me enough about basic baseball statistics to know that Ron's .302 lifetime average was pretty impressive. He wasn't in the

Yankees' lineup that day at Tiger Stadium, however, and in fact wasn't even listed among the Yankees players on the scorecard my dad had bought. Why wasn't he there? What had happened to him? My dad didn't know.

It wasn't until 1978, when he resurfaced with the Chicago White Sox, that I began to understand why Ron hadn't been a visible part of those storied Bronx Zoo squads of 1976 and 1977. And it wouldn't be until another 41 years later, when Ron and I first started discussing this book project, that I began to fully comprehend just how deeply intertwined Ron and Thurman's lives and careers had been.

Theirs was a classic baseball friendship—two men of starkly different personalities and backgrounds bonded together as teammates by their love of the game and their desire to compete at its highest level. They were the back-to-back No. 1 draft picks of baseball's most renowned franchise, and there were many who thought that "Munson and Blomberg" could one day have the same dynastic ring to it as "Ruth and Gehrig" or "Mantle and Ford." But while Thurman more than lived up to the team's expectations—leading the Yankees to three straight American League pennants and two straight World Series championships—a series of injuries caused Ron to completely miss the bus to the postseason Promised Land.

It's a painful truism that you often find out who your real friends are when life deals you a losing hand, and that can be especially true in the world of team sports, where superstition and resentment often result in the ostracism and isolation of a player who can't contribute due to injuries. And yet, the warm friendship that Ron and Thurman formed before their career paths cruelly diverged remained remarkably, wonderfully intact, even during the darkest days of Ron's Disabled List purgatory.

For many baseball fans and writers, the game is all about cold, hard numbers and the many fascinating things you can learn from crunching them. While I can certainly understand and appreciate that perspective, let me forewarn you that there won't be much number-crunching in the pages ahead. I've always been far more interested in the human side of the game, and the story you're about to read is a deeply human one indeed, filled with joy, sorrow, triumphs, mistakes, good deeds, bad pranks, and quite a few truly memorable characters.

This book is also not intended as a straight Thurman Munson biography; Marty Appel already covered that territory with his excellent *Munson: The Life and Death of a Yankee Captain*, so a detailed chronological recounting of Thurman's career and achievements would be rather redundant. Instead, imagine that you're sitting at your favorite bar—or, more appropriately, in a booth at your local delicatessen—with Ron as he shares robust recollections of his and Thurman's playing days, their adventures, and their friendship, while I occasionally pipe up with some helpful historical or cultural context.

Speaking of which, anyone who has read my previous baseball books knows that I'm as interested in the cultural context of the game as I am in the game itself, because baseball players are not robots who simply perform in a vacuum.

Thurman and Ron were teammates from 1969 through 1977, which means that they went through their respective ups and downs during a tremendously tumultuous period in both baseball history and American popular culture. In addition to shedding new light on Thurman's infinitely complex being, I wanted *The Captain & Me* to vividly take you back to the time in which he and Ron played, and give the reader a sense of what it was actually like to be a major league ballplayer in 1970s New York City—not just between the lines, in the dugout, and in the clubhouse, but also off the field and during the off-season.

While Ron and I were working on this book, I could always tell when he was about to unleash a particularly good anecdote: His Georgia accent would ramp up a notch or two, and he would excitedly preface the story with, "I'm never gon' forget!" While I had to edit out most of these exclamations for space purposes, I'm never gon' forget what a pleasure it was to work on this book with him. I truly hope you'll find it as much of a pleasure to read.

—Dan Epstein
Greensboro, North Carolina
October 2020

1

DHs and Deviled Eggs

It's April 6, 1973, and I'm sitting at my locker in the Fenway Park visitor's clubhouse, listening to the top of the second inning on the radio and eating deviled eggs.

"Bloomie! What the *eff* are you doing?"

I look up and see Thurman standing there in his catcher's gear. He does not look pleased.

"Thurman, there's deviled eggs over there," I tell him, excitedly pointing to the clubhouse spread. He looks over at the egg platters and instantly calculates that maybe half the eggs that were originally on them have already been eaten... by me. Steam starts coming out of his ears.

"You *can't* eat all those eggs!" he growls.

"C'mon, Thurman—I'll save ya a few!"

"No!" he barks, fixing me with a murderous glare. "If you're going to do this after every time you hit, there's not gonna be enough food left for any of us to eat after the game!"

On the radio, we can hear Roy White grounding out to end the inning, which is Thurman's cue to head back out to the field. But before he does, he grabs a paper plate, hurriedly loads it up with deviled eggs and kielbasa, and shoves it into the top shelf of his locker for safe keeping. He knows I love to eat, but he also knows I know better than to take food out of his locker.

Baseball history, my life, and the fate of that Fenway deviled egg tray all might have turned out a lot different, if only I hadn't pulled my hamstring during a spring training game about a week earlier. I was having a very good spring, playing first base and hitting the ball extremely well; and I was coming off a pretty good season in '72, so I knew I was going to break camp with the Yankees for the second year in a row as the team's starting first baseman.

But the hamstring thing was a problem. It didn't hurt so bad that I couldn't walk, but it was definitely getting in the way of my ability to run or field my position at first. Back then, when you pulled a hamstring, all they did was put ice on it for a couple of days, put you in the whirlpool, and give you some pills for inflammation. They didn't put you in the ice bath, do MRIs or any of that, and they had no way of telling how bad it was—it was just a hamstring pull.

Ralph Houk, who was our manager, called me into his office along with coaches Ellie Howard and Dick Howser before we broke camp. "How's your leg?" they asked me.

"I can hit," I said, "and I can run half-speed. I'm okay."

They were silent for a bit, and then Ralph said, "We don't know if we should put you on the Disabled List."

I sure didn't like the sound of that. If you go on the Disabled List, they've got to bring someone else in, right? Well, back then we had one-year contracts. And even though I was popular up in New York with the fans, the team still had to win—and I didn't want to be in a Wally Pipp/Lou Gehrig–type situation. There was a good first baseman down in Triple A named Tony Solaita, who had hit a bunch of home runs in '72, and I'm thinking to myself, "If I go on the DL, this guy could take my job."

We were scheduled to open the season against the Red Sox at Fenway. Luis Tiant was already penciled in to pitch, and he's a right-handed pitcher and I'm a left-handed hitter, so I told Ralph, "Don't put me on the DL—I can absolutely hit against Tiant!"

"It's going to be cold up there," he reminded me.

"I don't care," I said. "I can hit!"

Mobility would definitely have been an issue for me if I'd had to play first base with my pulled hamstring. But because of this new "designated hitter" rule that the American League was trying out in 1973, there was still a viable position for me on the team. None of the players thought much about this at the time; to us, the DH was basically a pinch-hitter for four at-bats, an experiment that probably wouldn't last more than a season or two. But better to be a DH than on the DL, right? Ralph knew I could still contribute as a DH, so he decided to keep me on the team.

After some exhibition games against the Mets in New Orleans and a couple of other Southern cities, we fly up to Boston for Opening Day. We check into the hotel and head to the ballpark, just like we always do. Thurman and I get down to the visitors' clubhouse at Fenway, put our uniforms on, and go over to look at the lineup card. It says, "Blomberg, DH" in the sixth spot, "Alou F., 1B" in the seventh, and "Munson, C" in the eighth.

Thurman doesn't say anything about me being the first DH in Yankee history or anything like that, and neither do I; we're both just thinking about the game we have to play today. We walk from the clubhouse out to the field, which at Fenway is like going through a sewer—you've got rats down there, dripping pipes, puddles of ice water with wooden planks over them, the whole thing—and take batting practice. It's really cold out, but I'm swinging and hitting the ball well.

Since I'm batting sixth, I don't figure I'll be hitting in the first inning, but Tiant is having trouble finding the strike zone today. The next thing I know, I hear Sherm Feller's voice saying

"Ron Blomberg, Designated Hitter" over the Fenway P.A., and I'm walking to the plate with two outs and bases loaded. I'm the first DH to make a plate appearance in an official major league game, but that doesn't even occur to me right now. It's just another trip to the plate for me—the only difference is, it's my first of the season.

Despite what I'd told Ralph, I hate hitting against Tiant. Everybody does, because he's got like a hundred different windups and release points, and you never really know what's coming. Obviously, I'd love to hit a grand slam off him in this situation, but I wait patiently for a pitch I can drive, a pitch I can knock in a couple of runs with. I foul off a couple of tasty-looking ones, taking the count to 3-2; I know Tiant knows I'm a good hitter, and I know he's going to try and get me to swing at something off the plate, because he's not going to risk throwing something right down the pipe to me with the bases loaded. Sure enough, the next pitch floats in wide of the plate, I lay off it, and the umpire calls, "Ball four!" Matty Alou scores from third to put us up 1–0, and I trot down to first. I never go up to bat with the intention of drawing a walk, but I'm happy to bring in a run and keep the inning going.

Felipe Alou, Matty's older brother, comes up next and hits a double, driving in two runs and sending me to third. That brings Thurman up, but he pops out to Carl Yastrzemski at first for the last out of the inning. I head over to first base, just like I normally do, but Felipe's already standing there. "What are you doing?" he says.

"I'm playing first," I tell him.

"No, I am," he laughs. "You're the DH!"

I go back to the dugout and sit down on the bench next to Elston Howard. I'm freezing—it's maybe 34 degrees out on the field, but it feels even colder in our tiny cement dugout. Bobby Murcer always keeps a hot water bottle with him on the bench to stay warm; he's out in center field right now, so I try it out, but it isn't helping me much. I figure I'm going to be frozen solid before my next at-bat comes around, so I say to Ellie, "I'm freezing, what do I do?"

"Well, you could sit here with me," he says, "or you could go into the clubhouse and stay warm."

It honestly hadn't even occurred to me.

I pick up my bat and head back to the clubhouse. There's not really enough room in there to take big practice swings, so I take a seat on the stool in front of my locker and try to shake off the cold. There are no TVs in the clubhouse, but somebody's got a transistor radio on, so I listen in as Red Sox announcers Ned Martin and Dave Martin call the game.

Vince Orlando, the Red Sox clubhouse guy, starts putting food out on our clubhouse table. Vince is notorious for having the worst food in the world; it's always hot dogs, kielbasa sausages, and cabbage, and it always just stinks up the place something awful. The food is already prepared ahead of time; Vince just takes it out of the freezer, puts it in the oven, and gets it ready for when the team comes off the field at the end of the game.

I'm taking some light swings, trying not to hit anything in the clubhouse with my bat, when I notice Vince putting out a tray of deviled eggs along with the usual hot dogs and kielbasa. And all of a sudden, I'm getting hungry! I know I'm probably not due up again until the third or fourth inning, so I go over to the table and put three or four deviled eggs on a paper plate, along with a kielbasa. I'm listening to the game, I'm warm, I'm eating—my favorite thing in the world to do, other than playing baseball—and I'm starting to think, "You know, this is really not all that bad!"

Vince's deviled eggs are actually pretty good, so I get back up and grab some more of them, and then some more. And that's when Thurman comes in and, much to his supreme annoyance, finds me stuffing my face.

When it's finally time for me to bat again, there are two outs in the top of the third, and the Red Sox are winning 5–4. It's still freezing outside, but now it's also sunny; and after sitting for two innings in a dimly lit clubhouse, it's so bright I can barely see. But I still manage to knock a single off Tiant—my first hit in my first official at-bat as a DH—and then go to second on a single by Felipe. Thurman comes up in the position to put us ahead with a home run, but Tiant gets him to ground out to Rico Petrocelli at third, and the inning's over.

Mel Stottlemyre, our starting pitcher, stops me as I'm heading back to the dugout. "Did you leave me any deviled eggs?" he asks, and the stern look on his face tells me that he's not kidding around. Thurman must have told him about seeing me eating them in the clubhouse. "Yeah, there's still a few left," I laugh.

"You better have left me some!" he yells over his shoulder as he takes the mound.

Having already given up a run in the first inning and four in the second, Mel now gives up another three in the third—Reggie Smith singles, Carlton Fisk doubles, Doug Griffin drives them both home with a single and makes it to second on the throw home. It's like Mel is not even thinking about pitching; he's too rattled and distracted by thoughts of me devouring the rest of the clubhouse spread. Thurman always makes wisecracks whenever he goes out to the mound; knowing him, he's probably been needling Mel, telling him something like, "You better hurry up and get these guys out, because Bloomie's gonna eat all the deviled eggs!"

Ralph takes Mel out of the game after the third—he stops to grab some deviled eggs before he hits the showers—and we wind up losing 15–5. There's still a ton of polish sausage on the table when we get back to the clubhouse, but now the spread is missing about 85 percent of the deviled eggs. But before anyone can give me any crap about it, I'm surrounded at my locker by at least a dozen reporters, all of them asking me, "What was it like to be the first DH?" We'd just lost the first game of the season in a blowout, and here these guys are acting like I won the World Series with a home run. All my teammates are looking at me confused, like, "What in the world are they talking to you about?"

None of them seem to understand what a big deal it is, and I don't either. Marty Appel, the Yankees' public relations director, takes my bat so he can send it to the Hall of Fame. I suppose I should feel honored, but I'm actually really upset; I knew when I picked the bat out that I was going to get at least 30 or 40 hits out of it, and now it's heading to Cooperstown before I've barely had a chance to swing it. Orlando Cepeda was in the Red Sox lineup today as their DH; if "El Tiante" had gotten Bobby Murcer or Graig Nettles out to end the first inning, rather than walking them right in front of me, Cepeda could have come up in the bottom of the first and gone down in history as "the First DH," and I'd have gotten to keep my bat. But that's baseball for you.

We've lost the ballgame, I've lost my bat, and I've eaten pretty much all the deviled eggs, much to the displeasure of several of my teammates. But the good news is, I've found a new position. To commemorate this historic day, Thurman sneaks my first baseman's glove out of my locker and decorates it with a magic marker while I'm busy talking to the reporters. I turn around just in time to catch him as he's sneaking it back in. The big, black letters he's written on the thumb read "U.S. Steel."

2

First Impressions

People think playing baseball is easy. They think you just put your uniform on, go out there, hit the ball, run around the bases, catch a few balls, and hope you win a ballgame. People think it's a kid's game.

What people don't realize is that you've gotta be good to be a star in high school baseball, and you've gotta be *real* good to be a star at any level of college ball. And then you've gotta be almost great to even be drafted by a major league team, because if you're drafted that means you were not only one of the best players on your team, but also in your league. When you play minor league baseball, these guys you're playing against are the best of the best of all high school and college teams. And only a very small percentage of those guys in the minors ever make it to the major leagues.

The big question with Thurman Munson and Ron Blomberg wasn't if they'd make it to the major leagues, but when. Ron had been drafted by the New York Yankees out of Atlanta's Druid Hills High School as the No. 1 overall pick of the June 1967 Amateur Draft, ahead of such future stars as Jon Matlack, John Mayberry, and Ted Simmons. The following year, Thurman—the first All-American baseball player in the history of Ohio's Kent State University—was the Yankees' first-round selection in the 1968 Amateur Draft, ahead of the talented likes of Greg Luzinski, Gary Matthews, and Bill Buckner. While a high draft pick number is never a guaranteed indicator of future success (the Astros, who had a chance to draft Thurman ahead of the Yankees, chose to go instead with a high school catcher named Martin Cott, who barely made it out of A ball), the Yankees' scouts and front office were extremely high on these two youngsters' future prospects.

I remember the day that Thurman signed with the Yankees. It was a big deal, because the Yankees were telling everyone that they had found their "catcher of the future." I was playing with the Kinston Eagles of the Carolina League at the time, in my first full summer of professional ball. I was struggling a bit—I'd signed for a big bonus, so there was a lot of pressure on me to justify it by hitting a lot of home runs, and I kind of messed up my swing for a while because of it—but I had no doubt that I was going to make it up to the big leagues. So I knew that Thurman and I would be teammates together before too long.

The Yankees certainly hoped so. After the dynastic post-WWII period of 1947 to 1964, where the team had won the American League pennant 15 times, the Bronx Bombers were now experiencing their deepest doldrums in franchise history. In 1966, they'd even finished 10th and last in the league, their first cellar-dwelling year since 1912, when the team was still known as the Highlanders. The Yankees clawed their way into ninth place in 1967, and even managed to get over the .500 hump and into fifth place in 1968, but the glorious days of pinstriped domination definitely seemed like a thing of the distant past—a past that seemed even more distant in the spring of 1969, when the legendary Mickey Mantle announced his retirement.

I was lucky to get drafted when I did. If the Yankees hadn't been so bad in 1966, they wouldn't have had the No. 1 pick for the '67 draft, and some other team might have drafted me before them. I didn't want to sign with any other team. If the Yankees hadn't drafted me, I probably would have gone to UCLA and played basketball for John Wooden, or played football for Bear Bryant at Alabama. I was a basketball and football star in high school as well as baseball, and both UCLA and Alabama were offering me scholarships to come and play for them. Those were two of the most exciting programs in college sports, so playing baseball for anyone other than the Yankees seemed pretty unexciting to me in comparison. I mean, I was kind of a Braves fan at the time, but that was only because I lived in Atlanta and they'd recently moved to town from Milwaukee. If they'd drafted me, I wouldn't have signed with them.

I'd grown up going to see a minor league team called the Atlanta Crackers, who played over at Ponce de Leon Park, which wasn't too far from where I lived. I was a big Atlanta Crackers fan. Nobody was talking about Major League Baseball down there at the time, and the only time we ever got to see Major League Baseball down there was on NBC's *Game of the Week*, with Pee Wee Reese and Dizzy Dean calling the games. The Yankees always seemed to be on *Game of the Week*, with their games being broadcast from the old Yankee Stadium. At the time, the Yankees had guys like Mickey Mantle, Roger Maris, Whitey Ford, and Yogi Berra. I saw them play some spring exhibition games in Atlanta on their way up to New York from Fort Lauderdale, and I became a Yankee fan. And then I started learning more about Yankee history, and understanding what an important team they were. Mickey Mantle became my hero; I would imitate his stance and his swing, and always ask to wear No. 7 on my little league and high school teams. So when the Yankees started scouting me, that was as exciting to me as being scouted by UCLA or Alabama.

The other thing that appealed to me about playing for the Yankees was New York City. I wasn't very religious, but I was always a proud Jew, and my family had always celebrated Hanukkah, Rosh Hashanah, and Yom Kippur. There weren't too many Jews down in the South back then, and the KKK and the John Birch Society were pretty active, and they didn't like Jews very much. But my parents told me that there were all these Jews in New York, and that was a big deal to me. The idea of playing ball in front of a lot of Jewish fans in New York was really exciting to me, and I knew that being a Jewish ballplayer in, say, Detroit or Cleveland or Kansas City or Houston wouldn't be quite the same thing. So when the Yankees drafted me, it was a no-brainer for me to sign with them.

The Yankees were excited about the idea of having a Jewish player, too. They weren't drawing a lot of fans to the ballpark in those days, and they knew having a Jewish star would be a good gate attraction for them and bring a lot of Jewish fans out to Yankee Stadium. Also, in those days, the team had kind of a reputation, unfairly or otherwise, for being anti-Semitic—just like they'd had a reputation for being racist, because it took them so long to sign a Black player—and signing a Jewish player would definitely help improve their image along those lines.

Of course, the Yankees also needed a great catcher, which is where Thurman came in. They'd won all those pennants and World Series with Yogi Berra and then Elston Howard behind the plate, but by the time Thurman and I came to training camp in '69, they had Jake Gibbs and Frank Fernandez splitting time as starting catcher. Both were good guys who were solid defensively—and Frank had some decent pop in his bat—but nothing about them exuded "greatness" in the way that Yogi and Ellie had. So when the teams in front of them passed on Thurman in the '68 draft, there was no question about who the Yankees were going to use their first pick on.

I always had the impression that Thurman would have been happy to sign with anybody who needed a catcher; he just wanted to get to the majors as quickly as possible. He'd also played football and basketball, but baseball was his number one sport, and he had total belief that he could excel on a major league level. He'd grown up in Canton, Ohio, and gone to school in Akron, so playing for the Indians would have been a natural thing for him. But Cleveland already had a really good defensive catcher named Joe Azcue, and a top catching prospect named Ray Fosse, so there wasn't a whole lot of interest in Thurman coming from that organization. But even if they had set their sights on him, the Yankees would have snapped him up before the Tribe's turn came around.

The Yankees drafted and signed Thurman in June of '68, and sent him off to play with the Binghamton Triplets, their AA team in the Eastern League, so we didn't actually meet until the following year, when we both went down to take spring training with the Yankees at their facilities in Fort Lauderdale. We hit it off pretty well, though we didn't hang out much together at camp that year. We were all really impressed by his skills—especially by how quickly he could get the ball out of his glove and down to second base. I'd never seen anyone get rid of the ball like that.

We both had good springs, and I got promoted to the Yankees' AA farm team in Manchester, New Hampshire, while they sent Thurman up to their AAA club in Syracuse, New York. They also got him into the National Guard, which they did for a lot of their players, me included. The Vietnam War was going on, and if you were a healthy guy of draft age who didn't have a college deferment, there was no way you were going to get out of serving. Bobby Murcer, who the Yankees saw as their successor to Mickey Mantle, had missed all of the '67 and '68 seasons because he was in the military. But the Yankees had a lot of connections that they were able to use to get a lot of players a deferment from the Vietnam draft by signing us up for National Guard duty.

Obviously it was better than being shipped off to combat overseas, but being in the National Guard was no picnic, especially when you had to do your meetings during the baseball season. In '68, when I was at Kinston, I had to do my basic training at Fort Jackson, South Carolina, and then would have to leave the team again every three weeks to go do my National Guard duty. And that's not easy to do. One of the other reasons I struggled in Kinston was that it seemed like every time I was getting on track I'd have to get on one of those puddle jumpers and fly down to Atlanta for Friday, Saturday, and Sunday. Then I'd fly back to whatever city we were playing in on Monday. And if you're hitting the ball well, taking three or four days off like that is murder; I really had a hard time adjusting to that. Thankfully, I had a good year in Manchester in '69.

Thurman only played 28 games for Syracuse in 1969 because of his National Guard duty, but still managed to hit .363 in limited action, while Ron hit .284 with 19 home runs in 107 games at Manchester. Thurman was called up to the Yankees on August 8, and immediately made his mark, going 2-for-3 with two RBIs in his first major league game, while catching Al Downing's 5–0 complete game shutout of the Oakland A's at Yankee Stadium. (That same night, Ron hit a pair of two-run homers to lead the Manchester Yankees to a 5–1 victory over the Elmira Pioneers.) Thurman was shipped back to Syracuse the following week, but both he and Ron—along with fellow

Yankee prospects Alan Closter, John Ellis, Ron Klimkowski, Steve Kline, Dave McDonald, Mickey Scott, Tony Solaita, and Frank Tepedino—were recalled in September.

The Yankees were not stockpiling bats and arms for the pennant race; the team had struggled all season to get above the .500 mark, and were already 25 games in back of the first-place Orioles by the beginning of September. Skipper Ralph Houk told the press that he intended to give Thurman substantial playing time over the last few weeks of the season, but that the rest of the September call-ups were mostly just there to get a taste of life in the major leagues.

The 1969 Yankees had a rising star in Bobby Murcer, who would hit 26 homers that season while performing impressively in right field. There was also the ever-dependable Roy White in left field, the speedy Horace Clarke at second, a couple of workhorse starting pitchers in Mel Stottlemyre and Fritz Peterson (who pitched over a third of the staff's combined innings and accounted for 37 of the team's 80 wins), and a solid closer in Jack Aker. Other than that, however, the team's roster seemed largely comprised of veterans whose better days were behind them, younger players who weren't living up to the team's expectations, and guys who were there simply because Houk occasionally needed an extra warm body or two to put in the lineup or the bullpen. And then there was Joe Pepitone, the team's last remaining star from its pennant-winning days, who hit 27 home runs in 1969—his highest total since 1966—but had become so disruptive a presence that the Yankees would trade him to Houston in December.

Joe Pepitone—you talk about a guy that should have been in the Hall of Fame. He had all the tools, he could play first base as well as anybody and cover a lot of ground in the outfield, but he was always more interested in doing his own thing. When we got called up to the team in September of '69, Joe had just returned from his "leave of absence"—we found out later that basically he was off on his boat, fishing. He was in a lot of debt, and was constantly haggling with the front office about money. He was the established star of the team, but he didn't want to be there.

I'd gotten to know Joe a little bit during the two spring trainings I'd been to with the Yankees. He would always talk to me, tell me stories and stuff like that, and half the time I never knew if he was kidding or not. I mean, he was just *out* there, always yelling at everybody and telling jokes, even when he was on the field. I couldn't go out with him at night, because I couldn't keep up with him—no one could! And when Joe went out at night, you had no idea if he would actually show up at the ballpark the next day. He was like a wild animal; if you let him loose in the jungle, you have no idea where he'll go. But when he was out on the field and focused, he was great. It was hard to stay mad at him, because when he actually played he would give you 120 percent; but if he gave you 120 percent in the first game of a doubleheader, he also might disappear before the second game started.

Joe was definitely the most colorful guy I ever played with. He was perfect for the disco era, with his hairdo and gold chains, only the disco era hadn't happened yet. He was "Mr. Charisma"—you walk into a club with him, and he's immediately got girls all over him and people wanting to buy him drinks. Even in spring training, he'd show up driving one of those Cadillac Eldorados that were like 60 feet long, with his whole entourage. And these guys, his friends who would come down to the clubhouse, you had to be careful what you said around them. They were the type of guys who, if they took something you said the wrong way, you'd wind up with both your legs broken, or your head would be found bobbing in the East River the next day.

Thurman liked Pepi, and would laugh at his jokes in the clubhouse, but he couldn't relate to him at all. Even as a rookie, Thurman was all business when it came to playing baseball. He lived to come to the ballpark every day. With Thurman, it was never a question of "I don't feel like it" or "I've got something better to do." And once he was on the field, he was deadly serious about playing and winning. Joe, on the other hand, would constantly joke around during the game, even on the field; if he could get a laugh out of the guys on the other team, he would. Thurman never said anything to him about it, because he was a rookie call-up and he knew it wasn't his place to do so. But sometimes you'd look over at Thurman while Pepi was going off on one of his tangents, and you could see him thinking, "What's *with* this guy?"

It was a stagnant time for the Yankees. They should have been going up, but they had a lot of not-great ballplayers, and it wasn't unusual to have only six or seven thousand people in the stands at Yankee Stadium for our games. CBS owned the Yankees at the time, and they did not want to spend a lot of money on the team, or make big trades that would help us win; they just saw it as a business operation. And this was right when the "Miracle Mets" were making their move to take over the NL East from the Cubs, so everybody in New York was talking about them. Woodstock had just happened upstate, as well, so that was the other thing everybody in the city was talking about. Compared to a historic Mets run and a historic concert, the Yankees were really kind of an afterthought.

I didn't play much that September, but it was still a real thrill to be taking batting practice or shagging flies at old Yankee Stadium. Not only had Babe Ruth and Lou Gehrig and Joe DiMaggio and Mickey Mantle and Whitey Ford and all those guys played there, but the stadium had played host to all kinds of historic football games and boxing matches and concerts and other big events; even the Pope had appeared there. For me, going to New York was like going to a different country, but "The House That Ruth Built" had that same feeling of history to me as I used to get from the Civil War battlefields in the South.

Thurman started just about every game we played that month; Ralph Houk wanted him to get comfortable with our pitching staff—and they with him—as soon as possible, instead of waiting for spring training to come around. He was only 22, a year older than me, but he took to the assignment like a seasoned veteran. He struggled a bit at the plate, but he had total confidence behind it. Established pitchers don't usually like to take orders from rookie catchers, but it didn't take long before he'd earned the respect of most of the pitchers on the staff for his ability to call pitches. The only pitcher I remember shaking him off a bunch was Steve Hamilton, our veteran reliever who was famous for his "folly floater" pitch. Steve had been pitching professionally since Thurman was a little kid, but that didn't faze Thurman one bit. "You throw what I *tell* you to throw," Thurman told him.

September 1969 was when Thurman and I really started to become friends. Thurman and I lived at the Grand Concourse Plaza in the Bronx, which was where the Yankees put up all the call-ups (a lot of the older Yankee players lived there, as well). It was just up the street from Yankee Stadium, so we'd just walk to the park together. And we started talking a little bit about where we were from and what our lives were like back home.

Atlanta was a big city by Southern standards, but it seemed pretty small compared to New York, and Thurman was from Canton, which was really small in comparison. I was a lot more outgoing and talkative than he was, but we realized that we were similar in a lot of ways. Neither of us had come from much money, and we'd both worked really hard to get as far as we'd come in baseball. But more than that, we were both guys who loved the outdoors, especially fishing. Neither of us were big "party" guys—Thurman liked to have a beer or two after the game, and I didn't drink at all—but both of us *loved* to eat.

Almost as soon as I got to New York that September, I started stopping by the Roxy Delicatessen, which was on 161st and Gerard in the Bronx, right underneath the L and just a few blocks from the ballpark. I became friends with the owners, and they would give me free food because I was Jewish *and* a Yankee. This was great, because I was making almost no money at the time, and I would have starved to death if I'd had to survive off the clubhouse spread.

Thurman and I would often walk back to the Grand Concourse Plaza after the game, and one night I suggested that we stop off at the Roxy for a bite on our way home. Thurman didn't know too much about Judaism or Jewish culture at the time; there was a small Jewish community in Canton, but I don't think he'd interacted with Jews too much. He was always talking about the White Castles he'd grown up eating in Canton, but Jewish delis hadn't been on his radar. The first time I took him to the Roxy, he tried to order a regular corned beef sandwich, but I stopped him.

"Thurman, here's what we're gonna do," I told him. "We're gonna get a platter of corned beef, pastrami, and brisket. And they're gonna bring us some bread, and they're gonna bring us some mustard, and they're gonna bring us some half-sour pickles and some sauerkraut, and you're gonna have a Dr. Brown's soda. You want some matzah ball soup, too?"

He had no idea what I was talking about. He'd never heard of matzah ball soup, never knew what a half-sour pickle was, never knew what a Dr. Brown's drink was. But you should have seen his face when they started bringing out the food to us, and you should have seen the way his eyes lit up when he sank his teeth into a big pile of pastrami and corned beef sandwiched between two slices of fresh rye bread. He was in heaven!

I got Thurman hooked on pastrami and corned beef, and on "the Mish-Mosh," which is chicken soup with noodles, kreplach, carrots, celery, and two big matzah balls. He couldn't get enough of it. From then on, for the rest of September, we'd be getting dressed after the game and he'd say, "Hey Bloomie— we going to the Roxy?"

And I'd say, "Of course!"

With the 1969 season officially a lost cause, Ralph Houk and the Yankees' front office already had their eyes on 1970 and beyond. Annoyed by the Mets' surprise success and the media attention they were receiving because of it, "the Major" (as Houk was known) told anyone who would listen that the Yankees were still the better ballclub, and that he was itching for a crosstown World Series in the next year or two where they could prove it.

When they bid each other farewell at season's end, Thurman was already a lock to be the team's starting catcher for 1970; but despite going 3-for-6 in limited play during his September call-up, Ron was still looking at spending another year or so in the minors. As sportswriter Bob Kurland wrote that fall in The Hackensack Record, "The Yanks are hoping that he'll be ready in 1971, the year they figure the Thurman Munsons and Blombergs will spark them to a pennant."

3

One Goes Up, One Goes Down

Thurman and I had a lot to catch up on when we met down at spring training in 1970. We were both big college football fans, so we talked a lot about what had happened at the end of the '69 college season. He still couldn't get over the fact that Ohio State, the No. 1 team in the country, had been upset by Michigan in November, breaking their 22-game winning streak and leaving them shut out from the bowl games. He liked to bet on college games, and I don't think he did too well on that one!

The biggest news Thurman had was that Diana, his wife, was pregnant with their first child, and was due to give birth sometime in April. Tough and gruff as he seemed on the surface, he was really over the moon about becoming a dad; it was like he would visibly soften into a giant teddy bear whenever the subject came up.

It was the same thing with Diana—or Diane, as he always called her. You could tell how happy she made him whenever he'd talk about her. They'd been sweethearts since high school, maybe earlier, and you got the sense that Thurman had known they would be together since the first time they'd met. As with any ballclub, the Yankees had some guys on the team that liked to chase girls, even if they were already married, but that was never Thurman's game at all. Spring training was prime time for checking out girls, too, either in the stands during our exhibition games or at the nightclubs afterward, but Thurman wasn't into that either. "You guys go have fun," he'd say. "Diane's the only one for me."

Thurman didn't like to talk much about his own family, and I got the impression pretty early in our friendship that he carried a lot of pain and hard feelings over their relationship. But he talked all the time about Diana and her family—it was like they'd adopted him, and he felt closer to them than to his own parents and siblings. He was especially close with Tote, Diana's dad, and I'd get to know Tote pretty well in the coming years.

For now, though, Thurman and I were staying at Schrafft's Motor Inn in Fort Lauderdale, which was the team hotel and was right on US 1, down by the beach. The Yankees put up all their players and coaches there during spring training, and unless you were married and had your family down with you—and I would say 75 to 80 percent of the people at camp didn't have their families with them—you had to have a roommate. Nobody had single rooms back then; we always had roommates, even on the road.

We shared rides, too. We trained at Fort Lauderdale Stadium, a.k.a. "Little Yankee Stadium," which was only about 15 minutes away from the hotel. Most of us couldn't afford to rent cars for the entire time we were at camp, so we would all pile into the handful of cars that the Yankees rented to take us to the park and back. It's not like nowadays, where the players all have their entourages and limousines. Sometimes even writers would go with us—a lot of them didn't have cars down there either—but it was understood that nothing we said in the car would end up in the papers; that stuff was always off-limits.

The first week of spring training was pretty relaxed. We'd be done with practice by like two o'clock in the afternoon, and then everybody would rush off to play golf or go fishing. Thurman and I were always in the fishing camp. Mel Stottlemyre always went fishing as well, and so did Curt Blefary, who the Yankees had gotten from the Astros over the winter in exchange for Joe Pepitone, and Frank Baker (a kid from Mississippi who was looking to make the team as a shortstop). A lot of Yankee players liked to fish, so we'd all go down to the Bahia Mar Marina, where we'd meet up with fishing guides. We'd get on like three or four different boats and we'd have fishing contests between the boats. Nobody had their own fishing rods, but the guides had fishing rods we could use. It was always a lot of fun.

Thurman and I would always be on the same boat, and we usually caught a few fish, but mostly we just enjoyed being out on the water, breathing the ocean air and shooting the breeze. We'd talk about fishing back home, our high school sports experiences, what it had been like for him playing at Kent State, what was happening in college basketball, just normal stuff like that. I was always a pretty talkative guy, and Thurman was kind of the opposite. But we genuinely liked each other, and felt a common bond developing between us, even though we had very different personalities. We just kind of gravitated to each other. It got to where we were kind of joined at the hip away from the ballpark. Whatever Thurman did, I did, and whatever I did, Thurman did.

We'd usually get back from the fishing trips at around five or six, go back to the hotel, take a shower, get dressed, and then a group of us would meet down in the lobby to go out to eat. Thurman, Stottlemyre, Roy White, and I really liked to go a place called Chateau Madrid, which was this restaurant in a big circular room up on top of a building that gave you a beautiful 360-degree view of Fort Lauderdale. But the really beautiful thing to us was their food. None of us made a lot of money, and Chateau Madrid was an all-you-can-eat restaurant. You could get shrimp, lobster, fish, steak, prime rib, everything you wanted, for $4.95. And I was a big eater, so any place where I could get a lot of food for not a lot of money was definitely my kind of place.

It was too good to be true, though. The third or fourth time we went there with our group, I got kicked out of the restaurant and they wouldn't let me come back, because I ate too much. I ate all the lobsters and the stone crabs and the shrimp I could pile onto my plate, and went back like 10 times. Even though he'd seen me in action at the Roxy back in the Bronx, Thurman couldn't believe how much I was eating; he and the guys were all kidding me that I should have brought a feedbag and put it over my head like a horse, so I wouldn't have to go back and forth! Hey, I'm a ballplayer, I'm hungry, and I'm not making much money. But after like my 10th trip to buffet, the Chateau Madrid manager came over to our table and told us that we were banned from ever coming back there.

The guys were pretty mad at the manager, but they were *really* mad at me for ruining such a good dining situation. Now we had to find another place for our dinners, but there was no place like Chateau Madrid. We ended up usually going to another place, right on Commercial Boulevard by the ballpark, called Wolfie's. Going there was kind of like going to the Roxy in New York, with all the bagels and corned beef and matzah ball soup. We used to just destroy our food; we'd have the Wolfie's waiters constantly going back and forth and back and forth.

Elston Howard went to Wolfie's with us a lot, too. Ellie and Thurman got along great, and they were always talking about catching. Thurman had a million questions for him about our pitchers and how to pitch to certain opposing hitters. Ellie

31

clearly appreciated the respect that Thurman showed for his knowledge and experience, and was always more than happy to share what he knew with him. Ellie was our hitting coach, but I don't think Ellie told Thurman a lot about hitting; he may have adjusted him a bit, but not much. Ellie really enjoyed catching, though, and he saw that same enjoyment in Thurman, so he took him under his wing right away.

After dinner, we would sometimes go out to the nightclubs, but usually we'd all go out to the jai alai places together, or the dog tracks. We'd bet like a dollar or two, nothing big, but it was something to do for a few hours rather than just go back to our hotel rooms. We'd get back at like 11:00 at night, and then we'd get up at 6:30 or 7:00 in the morning and go to the ballpark.

I had a super spring in '70, playing right field and first base, but it was pretty clear to everybody that I would be going to Syracuse when the season started. I wanted to go north with the Yankees, and even though I knew better, part of me hoped that maybe I could do well enough to impress Ralph and the coaches, and I'd make the team. But not too many people will win a position in spring training, unless they're a pitcher.

They already had Thurman penciled in at catcher, and he caught every single day in spring training that year. Everybody knew he had the ability and character to be the team's starting catcher, but it was like he showed up to camp fully formed, a veteran catcher in a rookie's body. The Yankees were overjoyed, because they'd put all their eggs in one basket when they drafted him; he'd gotten a big bonus to sign with them not even two years ago, and he was already good enough to be their everyday guy behind the plate. Jake Gibbs, who had been on the team's roster as a catcher since 1965, would be Thurman's backup. It wasn't like Thurman beat him out for the job, though; it was predetermined the previous fall that Thurman would have the job. And even Jake was impressed by Thurman's skills, savvy, and work ethic.

The Yankees had another young catcher in camp, John Ellis, who hit well enough that spring that he won the James P. Dawson Award, which is what they gave every year to the best rookie performance in spring training. Ralph decided to move him to first base, though, as a backup for Danny Cater; Thurman was just clearly the better all-around catcher. But since the team already had two first basemen and five outfielders—Blefary, White, and Murcer were the starters, and Jim Lyttle and Ron Woods were slated as backups—there was really no room for me on the roster, even if I'd hit .500 in camp. Like it or not, I was going to Syracuse for 1970. "Aw Bloomie, you'll be back in New York in no time," Thurman assured me, as I packed up my things in the clubhouse at the end of camp. "I'll buy ya lunch at the Roxy when you get there!"

Thurman, of course, turned out to be everything the Yankees were hoping for. He started 119 games at catcher in 1970, batted .302, threw out over half of the 64 runners who tried to steal a base on him, and won the American League Rookie of the Year Award almost unanimously. Thurman was the first AL catcher to win the prestigious award since it had been introduced in 1947, and the only catcher to win it other than the Cincinnati Reds' Johnny Bench, who'd won it in 1968. His future looked very bright, indeed.

On top of all that, Thurman helped lead the 1970 Yankees squad to a 93–69 record, their best since 1964. The team had no chance of catching the ridiculously loaded Baltimore Orioles, who finished with 108 wins and went on to win the World Series against the Reds, but they still finished in second place in the AL East. Their final wins total was also 10 games better than that of the crosstown Mets, which lent some credence to Ralph Houk's claim that the Yankees were actually the better of the two New York teams.

Despite Thurman's kind assurances, though, Ron never made it back to the Big Apple in 1970. No room ever opened up on the Yankees' roster for him; but far more frustrating for Ron was the fact that he didn't even get to play every day with the Syracuse Chiefs, the Yankees' AAA club in the International League. The team was helmed by longtime manager Frank Verdi, a minor league lifer who'd skippered the 1969 Chiefs to the International League championship and was determined to do so again. The Chiefs were well-stocked with veteran major leaguers and minor league journeymen in their late twenties and early thirties; the clock was running out on their careers, but they could still help

Verdi win now. At 21, Ron—the youngest member of the team—didn't really fit in with Verdi's vision; rather than put him in the lineup every day to give him as much experience as possible, Verdi determined that Ron would be more valuable to the team's push to win their second straight championship as a platoon player. It was a decision that would haunt Ron for the rest of his career.

Verdi really preferred to play the veteran guys, and I was the youngster, so I was the odd man out. I thought I was going to Syracuse to play and play and play, but Verdi had me playing only against right-handed pitchers. It made no sense to me; I could hit against anybody, right-handed or left-handed. The Yankees had signed me as their No. 1 draft pick, with a big bonus—and they weren't going to spend that kind of money on a guy who could only be a platoon player, right? But Verdi was trying to win every game; he wasn't really interested in player development, and he thought the Yankees would raise his salary if we won the championship again. I had a good year in '70, but it wasn't a great year, because I couldn't get in a day-to-day groove. And then word got back to the Yankees that I was only hitting against righties, which made them think that I couldn't hit lefties. The die was cast.

In some ways, the best part of '70 was seeing how well Thurman was doing with the Yankees. We communicated pretty regularly, maybe once or twice a month. I'd find out if the Yankees were on the road or not, and I'd call him up at his place and we'd talk. The first time I ever had White Castles was in Toledo, when I went there with the Chiefs to play the Mud Hens. Some of the older guys took me to a White Castle that was near the park, and I couldn't wait to tell Thurman that I'd had his favorite burger—actually, I had a lot of them—even though I would have much rather had some good pastrami and corned beef. I actually hit one of the longest home runs I ever hit in Toledo; it was like a bird snatched it out of the air and flew off with it! But other than that, Toledo was not a favorite place; those miles on the bus from Syracuse to Toledo and back were pretty miserable.

I'd always look at the newspapers and *The Sporting News* for the Yankees' box scores, and for any articles I could find on Thurman. It made me so proud to see him making a name for himself as a great catcher, and to read interviews with the Yankees' pitchers talking about how much they loved pitching to him. Stan Bahnsen, especially. Stan had already won Rookie of the Year in '68, but then he had a rough year in '69. When Thurman came up with the team in '70, he worked with

Stan on his control and got his ERA down from 3.83 to 3.33. Obviously, the Yankees did really well that year, but I saw from Stan what a difference Thurman could make for the team's staff. I just hoped that I would get a chance to see him make that difference in person in '71.

4

This Time It's for Real

Spring training was a lot different back then. In those days, you would go down to spring training to get into shape; nowadays, you have to show up at spring training already *in* shape. Most of the regular guys played a lot of innings in spring training, and Thurman was one of them. He caught a lot of innings not just to get in shape, but to get back in sync with the pitchers on our staff. And if you were a pitcher who came down to spring training with the Yankees for the first time, you were definitely going to be working with Thurman. He taught a lot of these guys how to really pitch; you could see that leadership, even in spring training. He really took an interest in working with the young arms.

Thurman brought Diana and their little daughter down to spring training with him in 1971, and they weren't staying at Schrafft's with the rest of us, but we still hung out a bit together off the field. That was the first time I met Diana. She was quiet, a beautiful lady and a really nice person and you could tell that Thurman and her were very, very close. I think that was also the first time I met Tote, his father-in-law. I had no idea who he was when I first saw him hanging around with Thurman in the clubhouse; he was this short, stocky guy with slicked-back hair. I asked Elston Howard, "Ellie, who is that guy with Thurman?"

"Oh, that's Thurman's father-in-law," he said.

Nobody knew too much about Tote. He ran a pool hall back in Canton—which was probably how Thurman got so good at pool—and while he wasn't a gangster, you might make that assumption from the way he looked and talked. But he was a really fun guy. Unlike Thurman, he was really pleasant and outgoing with everybody, and everybody loved him. Tote and I became friends pretty quickly; like Thurman, he was big into college football, and we'd talk about that all the time.

Thurman and Tote were really tight; they just loved each other so much. People always talked about how gruff Thurman was, because that's how he looked on the baseball field, and that's how he seemed in interviews. But they don't realize how soft and loving he was with his family, how much he loved Diana and his kids, and how much Tote was like a father to him. His own father really did not present a great role model to Thurman, and that's why Tote was so important to him. People didn't see that part of his life, but I did.

Tote's presence in the clubhouse was unusual, because in those days we didn't have a lot of guests in there with us. It's not like going to the ballpark nowadays, where players have their financial people, their food people, their fitness people with them. The only thing we had was us—us and the writers.

Thurman had only been in the big leagues for a single year at this point, but his distaste for writers was already fully developed. He never told me if there was a particular thing that happened that made him feel this way, but he had no patience with doing interviews, and no trust in most of the writers. I'll never forget one time in Fort Lauderdale that spring: We were in the clubhouse, and Dick Young started asking Thurman all these questions, like "Why this? Why this? Why this?" Thurman didn't say anything, but he got up from his seat by the lockers and started slowly backing Dick Young into the corner. He looked like he was about to kill him! Dick Young kept saying, "I just need to get some information," but Thurman didn't say a thing until he had him completely backed up against the wall, with their faces just a couple of inches from each other.

"Don't you ever ask me *anything*," Thurman hissed at him. "I don't like writers. I don't talk to writers. Don't ask me questions."

"I'm just doing my job," Dick insisted.

Thurman thought about this for a second, and told him, "Then I'm just going to give you one-word answers. Because whatever you say in your column, it's never the truth."

Everything in the clubhouse stopped, and everybody was looking at them. At that time, Dick Young was *the* guy in New York. He had a big column in the *Daily News*, and in *The Sporting News* too. You just didn't go up against this guy. But Dick pretty much avoided him after that. He wouldn't ask him many questions, and he was always real careful to gauge Thurman's mood before asking.

Thurman was grumpy when he was in the clubhouse. That's just how he was. Before he got to the stadium, he was wonderful. But as soon as he parked his car, walked into the stadium and into the clubhouse, his whole demeanor would change. It was Dr. Jekyll and Mr. Hyde, a totally different personality. While he was in the clubhouse, he just did not want to be bothered.

Thurman's attitude was that he should feel safe when he was in the clubhouse. If you wanted to write about what he did on the field, he looked at it as fair game. And he was often willing to talk to writers on the team plane, or in the hotel lobby, at least the ones that he liked. But when he was in the clubhouse, it meant he was either gearing up for a game or winding down from one, and he didn't want to deal with questions from reporters. "When you are in the clubhouse, this is *my* house," he explained to me once. "I do what I want to do, and I talk to who I want to talk to. And if I want to get in someone's face, I get in someone's face."

The clubhouse in Little Yankee Stadium was like one big room. That was the first place I ever saw somebody get the hotfoot, and it was Thurman who did it. A reporter (I can't remember which one) was talking to a player, and I saw Thurman sneak up and put a piece of chewed bubblegum on the reporter's shoe, and then stick a match into the bubblegum and light it. The reporter didn't notice what was happening, and then all of a sudden he looked down and saw he had a hole burning in his shoe! He started stomping on the flames with his other foot, looking like he was doing some kind of crazy dance, and everyone cracked up.

Thurman definitely had his devilish side, and I would see him and Fritz Peterson—the biggest prankster on our team—pull that trick a lot over the next few years. Unlike Fritz, though, Thurman wasn't the kind of guy who'd laugh loudly and let you know that he'd pranked you; he'd just go on about his business, like nothing had happened.

Writers weren't the only ones scared of Thurman; young pitchers, especially ones who were shy or introverted, would be scared to death of him when they first met him in camp. But he was always great with them. He would calm them down and help them focus; he knew that a lot of rookies were nervous when they came to camp or came up to the big leagues for the first time. *He* had been nervous when he came up to the big leagues, but he never forgot how Jake Gibbs had helped him settle in. And he felt that it was part of his job, both as a catcher and a team leader, to help get the young pitchers on track.

Once again, Ron found himself heading back to Syracuse when the Yankees broke camp in 1971. Frank Verdi had quit the Chiefs in the off-season, angry that that the Yankees hadn't raised his salary despite him managing the team to two straight International League championships. The Yankees replaced him with Loren Babe, another minor league lifer, who had led the Chiefs in hitting back in 1952. Babe continued playing Ron along the platoon lines set by Verdi, but the young outfielder hit so well during the first half of the season—.326 with nine doubles, six homers, and 20 RBIs in 48 games, while walking 19 times and striking out only 12—that the Yankees sent him a ticket to the Bronx on June 24.

The Yankees team Ron joined had not been able to keep the momentum of the 1970 squad rolling into the new season. On June 24, the team was 32–37 and battling the lowly Cleveland Indians for fourth place in the AL East, 13 games behind the first-place Baltimore Orioles. With the exception of Bobby Murcer, who was tearing up the league with a .337 average, the Yankees were particularly deficient in the hitting department. Thurman, who was virtually flawless in the field (he'd made what would be his lone error of 1971 about a week before Ron was called up), was one of the many Yankees struggling at the plate, his average bobbing at about 50 points below his .302 mark from 1970. The team hoped that Ron's potent bat would add some pop to their offense, and that his presence on the field would shore up their faltering attendance. "One doesn't accent ethnic situations these days," wrote Joe Trimble of the Daily News *when Ron was called* up, *"but it can't do the Yankee Stadium turnstiles any harm to have a Jewish player of distinction in the Bronx."*

It was so exciting to finally get called up to the team. Pete Sheehy, the Yankees' legendary equipment manager, showed me to my new locker—three down from Thurman's—where my new pinstripes were hanging. "Bloomie, you made it!" shouted Thurman, giving me a big hug.

I wasn't the only "new guy" to arrive that day. The Yankees had also picked up Ron Swoboda, who'd they'd got from the Montreal Expos for Ron Woods. This was a big deal, because "Rocky," as everybody called Swoboda, had been a hero with the Mets in the World Series in '69, and everybody remembered that great catch he'd made against the Orioles. Of course, Rocky played right field and batted from the right-hand side, so it was pretty clear that the Yankees were going to platoon me with him. It was a situation that wasn't ideal for either of us, but we got along great from the start. Rocky was a very serious guy, very opinionated. Whenever you'd ask him a question, he would give you a dissertation about the whole thing. If I had a bad game, he'd come up to me and tell me I should have done this, I should have done that, whatever. He wasn't doing it to rag me or embarrass me, and he would never do it in front of the team; Rocky just genuinely wanted to help me find my feet in the big leagues, and he was really generous with his knowledge.

Thurman was the same way, always super-encouraging to me, especially when I had not-so-great games. Shortly after I came up, we lost both ends of a doubleheader against the Indians at Yankee Stadium, on a day in which I mustered one measly hit, and made two errors—one in each game—that both led to the Indians scoring. I felt really crummy by the end of the day. "Let it go, my friend," Thurman told me in the clubhouse, when he saw my long face. "Everybody has bad games, even up here. We'll get 'em tomorrow." Sure enough, I went 3-for-4 the next day with a double and drove in two runs, and we beat them 9–2.

I quickly found out, however, that it didn't work the other way. If Thurman was struggling, you *never* said anything to him about it, especially if he was in a batting slump. The last thing he wanted to hear was "You'll get him next time, Thurm!" It was like waving a red flag at a bull, especially if he'd already gone 0-for-10 or something. Thurman's major thing was being a .300 hitter, and it really ate him up that he could never seem to lift his average over .250 in '71. But even though he might throw his batting helmet when he got back to the dugout, or go up into the tunnel and break his bat, he always made sure to do it far enough away from everybody, so you wouldn't get hit by his helmet or chunks of wood from his bat. And he never took it out onto the field with him. He might break his bat in two in frustration after popping out to the catcher with a runner on third, but when it came time for him to put his gear on again he'd be fully ready to catch and call the game. It was like he had everything completely compartmentalized. He may have been frustrated and angry with himself about how he was swinging, but he wasn't going to allow it to distract him from guiding his pitcher through the inning, or throwing out someone who was trying to steal on him.

A lot of people think of Thurman as hitting in the three-spot, but in '71 he mostly hit second. Ralph Houk would usually have Horace Clarke in the leadoff spot, or sometimes Jerry Kenney, and then put Thurman in the second spot. Thurman didn't strike out a lot, and he made good contact; and if he came up with a guy on second base, you knew there was a good chance he was gonna drive him in. I truly believe that Thurman was as good a hitter in the two-hole as Willie Randolph was for the Yankees later on.

Thurman was also pretty fast, which a lot of people don't remember. He had kind of a pudgy, Humpty-Dumpty type body, but he was actually a great all-around athlete, maybe even the second-fastest guy on the team behind Horace. Thurman could beat out a ground ball for a single. Thurman hit a lot of doubles, too, because he was a gap-to-gap hitter, and sometimes it was his speed that got him to second as much as where he'd hit the ball. And I don't think there was a catcher in baseball who could go from first to third as quickly as he could.

If we were not hitting the ball well, Thurman and I would show up at the ballpark a half an hour early and take batting practice. In those days, we didn't have films of our swings to examine, and we didn't have analytics to refer to. Maybe analytics would have helped us some, but Thurman and I were both natural hitters—and if you're a natural hitter, thinking can actually really mess you up. When a baseball is coming at you at a hundred miles an hour, you can't take your eye off the ball even for a millisecond, or you're never going to hit it. And if you start really thinking about it, you're done.

Thurman and I approached hitting a similar way. Every time we went up to the plate, we'd absorb the experience. There were only eleven other teams to play, and we'd play the teams in our division 18 times over the course of the season, so over time you got pretty familiar with the different pitchers in the league. After a while, I would know a pitcher. I would know how he threw to me in the first inning. I would know how this pitcher threw to me in the eighth, and if we're losing 2–1 and a man's on first base, I knew what I'm going to be looking for. Every time I get up to bat, I know I'm going to see one good pitch. And if I'm a good hitter, I'm going to hit that pitch three times out of 10 for base hits. And those other seven times, I might hit the ball well for five of them, but they'll be right to somebody. I can't tell you how many times Thurman or I would get two or three hits one day, and then we'd go 0-for-4 the next day, even though we'd hit the ball much harder than the day before.

What I quickly realized, watching Thurman play every day, was that he had the same kind of ability to absorb, analyze, and store information on opposing hitters. Thurman was like a computer in pinstripes. He knew every little detail of how these guys moved, what their strengths and weaknesses were, and he could recall it easily. That was part of what made him so invaluable to our pitching staff, and to our team; he was like a general who instinctively knew what strategy to follow in any given situation.

Back then, they would always have a player in the dugout charting the pitches for each game. They would keep track of what the pitchers threw, when they threw it, and how the hitters did on each pitch. The pitcher who was pitching the next day was usually the one who would do that, just to get his mind in the game. The team would then copy those charts and make them available to look at in the clubhouse before upcoming games, but Thurman didn't look at them much. He didn't have to.

Thurman loved to talk about hitting, at least when he was hitting well, and we'd often discuss opposing pitchers, especially the ones we had trouble with. Pete Broberg was the first guy I faced when I got called up to the Yankees in '71. He was a rookie, too; he came up to the Senators as a real glory boy, who'd gone straight from college to the majors. The Athletics had drafted him out of high school ahead of Thurman in '68, but then he went to Dartmouth and the Senators drafted him in the first round in '71. He threw hard, probably around 100, and everybody was talking about how fast this kid was. I hit my first major league home run off him, at Yankee Stadium, in my first game up with the team, and I hit another home run off him the following year. But that was it—I never got so much as a hit off him again. And Thurman went 0-for-16 lifetime against him. It always surprised me that Broberg didn't have a better career, because Thurman and I couldn't do anything against him.

Joe Coleman of the Tigers was another guy who really gave Thurman fits. You don't hear too much about him these days, but Coleman was really tough; he threw extremely hard, had a great sinker and a hard fastball, great changeup and a good curveball, but that heavy running fastball was especially tough to hit. Thurman caught it a few times and hit it out of the park, but most of the time he struggled against Joe. He was nasty, and he would go after your head in a second. All the right-handers hated to hit off him. There was no separate bullpen at Tiger Stadium; the pitchers warmed up on the field in foul territory. We'd see Coleman warming up out there before the game, and Thurman would groan, "Oh, no… I'm gonna have another tough game with this guy!"

One great pitcher that Thurman hit really well against was Bert Blyleven. I didn't do so well against him; first time I ever faced him, in July '71, he struck me out three times. He had a fastball in the high 90s, but he also had the best curveball I've ever seen, by far. He had such a sharp spin on the ball, you could actually hear it snapping when it was coming at you. That's what got him into the Hall of Fame, that curveball.

But Thurman was better at waiting for his pitch against Blyleven than I was. I remember Ralph telling me that the scouting report said Bert had super fastball and great curveball, and do *not* swing at the curve. And, you know, stupid me.... The only time you're gonna hit a curveball is when a pitcher hangs it; a good breaking pitch, especially one like Bert's, you're not gonna hit it. Ralph said, "Don't swing at his curveball, because his curveball is his out pitch." And of course I swung at his curveball and struck out three times. He had great stuff. He was the best pitcher I ever faced.

Bobby Murcer was the team's kingpin at the time I joined the team, and he and Thurman were already very tight by then; his wife, Kay, was also very close with Diana. Mickey Mantle had been my idol growing up, but Bobby was the one who was really supposed to be "the next Mickey Mantle." He'd even come from Oklahoma, same as Mickey. And like Mickey, Bobby hit some long home runs at old Yankee Stadium, and he could roam pretty good in that huge center field. Bobby was kind of captain of the outfield. When I came up in '71, I usually played in right, and Bobby would help me out. When a ball would be hit out to right-center, I would always listen for that great Oklahoma twang of his, calling me off or saying it was mine to take.

Bobby was a little bit quieter than Thurman was. When Thurman got mad, you would know it, but Bobby kept everything within himself. He was a very polite gentleman, and he always gave the right answers to the press; he was great with them, great with the fans, and people loved him. But Bobby would get mad like anybody else; he just used to hold it in. Thurman would swear and break stuff when he was mad, or dump everything out of his locker, but if Bobby struck out or popped out in a key situation, you only knew it was really killing him because you could see the veins sticking out on his neck.

Bobby was definitely one of the leaders of those early-70s Yankees teams, but he wasn't the type to get in your face if you messed up. Not a lot of the ballplayers would; that was Thurman's job. If you didn't run hard to first, if you missed an opportunity to take an extra base because you weren't paying enough attention, if you didn't barrel into the opposing team's catcher at the plate, he would get right in your face about it. You'd have spit all over you, but you wouldn't say anything back except maybe, "I'm sorry, Thurman, you're right!" Because 99.9 percent of the time, he was right.

Ralph Houk was never the type of manager who would say something directly to a player if he messed up. You could tell when he was upset, but Elston Howard was the guy on the coaching staff who actually delivered the message. Ellie always knew when Ralph was upset, and he'd take you aside and tell you why. If a ball dropped between two fielders because they were each expecting the other to go after it, it would be, "You guys need to communicate out there." If you were on base, you had to watch the ball; you couldn't just put your head down and run—you had to pay attention out there. And if you weren't doing that, it would be Ellie or Thurman who would take you aside. Thurman might say it more loudly than Ellie, but both of those guys took care to move you out of earshot of the rest of the bench before they gave it to you. The other guys might see Thurman talking to you, but they wouldn't know what he was saying. He didn't want to show anybody up; he just wanted you to play the game right.

The '71 Yankees weren't a great team, but it was a great bunch of guys, and we were close. Horace Clarke was one of the many characters on the team; we called him "Hoss." Even today, people will say to me, "Oh god, you played in the Horace Clarke Era," like that's a bad thing. But what a great guy, and he was a good ballplayer. People always laughed at Horace, because Horace was a small guy, around 5'9", and he always wore knee pads under his uniform pants, and he would wear his batting helmet when he was out in the field. Some people just look good in a uniform, but Horace didn't. His uniform was loose fitting, and he had a funny batting stance, both right- and left-handed. But Horace always, always played, even when he was injured, and his uniform was always dirty by the end of the game.

Hoss got the job done at second base, he just wasn't flashy about it. And he was great about handling Thurman's throws to second. When Thurman used to throw to get a runner, he rarely threw overhand. Ninety percent of the time he threw it submarine or sidearm, to get that quick release. And when you do that, your ball tails to the right. It would be going right into the runner as he was sliding in, and Hoss would get his glove right where it needed to be and tag the guy out.

Make no mistake—Horace had his fans, too. People in New York love a winner, but they also love an underdog, and if they see you giving 120 percent, they'll love you for it. They talk about the "Horace Clarke Era" because he was there for all those bad years, but the losing wasn't his fault. CBS didn't want to spend the money to make that team any good. We didn't have any superstars. Bobby Murcer was the closest to a superstar we had at the time, him and Thurman. And we had Roy White, a really good everyday ballplayer who could produce consistently at the plate. But we didn't have enough guys who could produce consistently at the plate to really take us all the way. We just weren't on that level yet.

Mel Stottlemyre and Fritz Peterson were our two best pitchers on that staff, and Fritz was probably the biggest prankster on the team. If you wrote a book about great baseball pranksters, there'd be a whole chapter devoted to him. He was a brilliant guy, and he'd always find clever ways to mess with people. He once sent Moose Skowron a fake letter from the Hall of Fame, asking Moose if he would donate his pacemaker to the Hall when he died. It looked completely official, and Moose was completely pissed about it. Elston Howard was one of Fritz's biggest victims, because Ellie would fall for anything. One time, Fritz and Mel and Stan Bahnsen found one of those order forms for encyclopedias, where you could order a whole set of books and they'd bill you later for them. Well, these guys ordered like 20 sets for Ellie, which was like 400–500 books, and had them all sent to him at Yankee Stadium. And Ellie was all excited when he saw all the boxes of books waiting for him, figuring that someone had sent them to him as a present, but he was a lot less excited when he got billed for all of them.

Fritz used to organize hockey games in the clubhouse, after Ralph and the coaches and all the reporters were gone, and there'd just be a few people left. They'd set up goals on either end of the clubhouse, tape up a ball like a puck, use bats as hockey sticks, and go nuts. If you came to the stadium early the next day, you could always tell if there'd been a hockey game, because they'd have bruises and black eyes, chairs would be broken, and half the stuff from your locker would be on the floor. They'd check each other into the lockers, and stuff would go flying. There would be blood all over the place, too. Fritz, Steve Kline, Stan Bahnsen, Mike Kekich, Mel Stottlemyre, Freddy Beene—those were the guys who really got into it, but other guys would play, too. You'd know if they were gonna play hockey, because they'd always play in their uniforms. Everybody else would already be showered and getting dressed, and they would still be hanging out in their uniforms, waiting for everybody to go home so they could start their game.

Like Thurman, Fritz was all business on the field, and he totally trusted Thurman to call the game for him. But off the field, the two of them often got up to mischief together. The Yankees always used to play the Army team in an exhibition game every year. We would get dressed at Yankee Stadium and then all take a bus up to West Point. We would eat with the cadets before the game, and they had a gorgeous, Olympic-sized swimming pool by their mess hall. One time when we were there, Fritz bet Thurman that he wouldn't jump into the pool from the upper deck of the mess hall, which was like 50 feet high; and the next thing you know, Thurman was cannonballing into the pool with his uniform on. He made a major splash, and the plebes went nuts. Ralph started yelling at Thurman, "If you get injured, we don't have a catcher!" But Thurman just laughed… and he played the ballgame soaking wet.

Thurman was a good golfer, and he used to keep his golf clubs at the stadium. One day in '71 we got to the park early and he decided that he and I should have a driving contest. We teed up the balls at home plate to see how far we could knock them. The only rule was that we couldn't use a driver; we had to use a two or three-iron. And we were hitting balls out of the ballpark; we each hit maybe 40–50 balls out onto the Grand Concourse. I guarantee someone called the cops to see where all these golf balls were coming from, but nobody ever said anything to us. A couple of them hit the scoreboard, and you could see the light bulbs shatter. It was so much fun!

The main targets of Thurman's pranks, of course, were the writers. Joe Trimble, who worked for the *Daily News*, would always bring his typewriter to the ballpark in a little suitcase. Joe was an older man and he would drink an awful lot up in the press box, and Thurman would always take his typewriter and hide it as he was trying to leave the clubhouse after the ballgame was over with. Trimble used to fly with us all the time, and Thurman used to give him the hotfoot on the plane. And he was so sauced-out a couple of times on the plane, Thurman would just grab his typewriter and sneak off with it, and Trimble wouldn't know where it was when he woke up. He would always get it back in the end; somebody would see him panicking and take pity on him and give it back to him. Sometimes, Thurman would mess with guys out of affection—like Jim Ogle of the *Newark Star-Ledger*, who was the only beat reporter that Thurman really got along with. But Thurman would always jump down Trimble's throat whenever Joe would try to interview him.

You could sometimes hear the writers talking among themselves about Thurman, saying "He's arrogant, he's gruff, he's mean," stuff like that. Because if Thurman didn't want to give an answer, which was most of the time, he'd just walk away, walk right past them. The writers were not allowed to go into the training room in the clubhouse, and the recreation room—where we had a pool table and a ping-pong table and drinks—was off-limits as well. So if Thurman was trying to avoid talking to the writers after the game, he would go into the training room and stay there, or go sit in the whirlpool or drink some beers for a while. The writers would be sitting there at his locker, just sitting there waiting for him to come out and give them some quotes, but he wouldn't come out. And if he did come out and say something to them, it would be one-word answers, or a sarcastic type of quote.

Fritz would talk to the writers; he hated them, too, but at least he would talk to them. And Thurman would occasionally talk to Murray Chass or Maury Allen, older guys who he had more respect for. But if a young beat writer came in from a Connecticut or New Jersey paper, or one of the local guys from Detroit or Boston came into our clubhouse when we were on the road and tried to talk to him, Thurman might start yelling at them. He would never hit anybody or anything like that, but he was very rude and abrupt, and could make these people feel real uncomfortable. He'd be walking around in his underwear and a ratty t-shirt, looking like he hadn't shaved for a week, giving them one-word answers or saying things like "Why are you asking me that question?" or "Get out of my way!" It didn't make him look like a good guy, but he didn't care. And then the writers might write some not-so-nice things about him in the papers because of his behavior, and that would give him all the more reason to not talk to them.

Me, I would talk to anybody. When they finally called me up to the team for good, it was a whole big thing; there weren't that many Jewish players in baseball—Kenny Holtzman, Mike Epstein, and Art Shamsky, that was pretty much it—and it was a big deal in New York that the Yankees finally had a Jewish player. The publicity was incredible. Every rabbi in the Tri-State area started contacting the team, wanting me to do this and that for their congregations. And before the games the Yankees would always have me come out on the field and say hello to Jewish groups who had come to the ballpark; there would be all these school groups, all these little kids with yarmulkes on, who were there to see me play.

Because I was such a novelty, I was in the papers all the time—"Blomberg did this, Blomberg did that"—and even if I didn't do anything in the game, the writers would come up to me in the clubhouse and ask me things, because they knew I was good copy. I would often sit and talk with Jim Ogle or Murray Chass on the team flights. Those guys were great about only writing things in the paper that they'd heard at the stadium; if I played some pranks during the flight or they overheard me joking around with some of the other guys, they wouldn't put anything about it in the paper.

Some of the guys on the team were a little jealous of me, because they'd been playing for six or seven years and now all of a sudden there's this glory boy who's only been with the team for a month or two, and everybody wants to talk to me. The Stage Deli down on 7th Avenue even named a sandwich after me: "The Ron Blomberg," which was a triple-decker with pastrami, corned beef, a Bermuda onion, and chopped liver. I always thought chopped liver was disgusting, so I could never actually eat it.

A lot of guys didn't understand why I liked talking to the writers, but Thurman never had a problem with it. He understood that I'd always been an extroverted person, and he never gave me any crap about who I was, or that I liked to talk to the press or anybody else. Thurman respected me for who I was.

When I first came up to the Yankees in '71, I bought a used Oldsmobile Toronado from a friend of mine, a total pimp car. Thurman used to get in it and ride with me when I'd go down to the Stage Deli, and sometimes we'd go down to the Garment District, as well. I would meet guys at the ballpark who'd invite me to come down to their shops in the Garment District, and Thurman and I would go down there the morning before a night game and they'd load us up with suits and shirts and pants and shoes. We'd sit down with the owners of the companies and sign autographs, and they loved us so much that they used to give us anything and everything we wanted. Thurman and I would come back to the clubhouse carrying all these brightly-colored leisure suits with crazy-patterned shirts, which was funny because Thurman never liked to dress flashy; he had this one plaid sport coat that he wore pretty much everywhere. But as long as they were giving us clothes, he thought it would be rude to refuse!

Thurman really loved going to the Stage Deli, though. That's where I got Thurman into knishes. When we would go to the Stage, knishes were always part of what they'd bring out to the table for us. Like a lot of places we went to, they wouldn't even bring out a menu for us— they'd just say, "We're gonna bring you a little bit of everything." So we'd sit down, and out would come the knishes, the bread, the pickles, the potato salad, the coleslaw. They'd always bring corned beef and brisket out there for us, and those big, thick french fries they had. The Stage owners used to sit down with us, and they'd bring their friends over to meet us. There were always actors and actresses there, people from the Broadway shows who wanted to meet us. The Stage owners took real good care of us, and they never charged us. And before we'd leave, they'd pack up a big cheesecake for us to take back to the guys in the clubhouse, because they knew our clubhouse spreads didn't have much that anyone would actually want to eat.

If all you knew about Thurman was what you read in the papers, you'd probably figure that he hated these kind of lunches, hated shaking hands and talking with people while he was eating, hated being recognized. He certainly wasn't a "look at me" kind of guy, and if you saw him walking into a restaurant, and you had no idea who he was, you would have no idea that he was an elite professional athlete. He just looked like a regular guy, the kind of guy you'd see getting a hamburger at White Castle or a pair of pants at Sears. He never made a big deal about showing up someplace, never acted like he was somebody special.

But the Thurman that I saw in these situations was the total opposite of the guy I saw playing hardnosed on the field or barking at writers in the clubhouse. Outside of the ballpark, he was totally relaxed, and totally personable. Walking around the streets of Midtown, people would recognize us and come up and talk to us, and Thurman would be great with them; he'd talk to them, shake their hands, sign autographs for them. Cab drivers would honk their horns at us and yell our names, and Thurman would wave and shout back. And when we were at the Stage Deli, it was like he was an honorary Jew. The Jewish patrons would come over to our booth because they recognized me, and then they'd see Thurman there, and they'd welcome him like he was an old friend or long-lost member of their family. They'd tell us jokes, talk about their kids, and give us their opinions on what the Yankees should be doing. It may have been a little bit of a culture shock for Thurman at first, but he loved it; the Jewish community really embraced him, and he embraced them back. He was tough as nails on the field, but off the field, he could schmooze with the best of them.

When we'd get back up to Yankee Stadium, there would always be kids and various other people waiting outside the players' entrance for autographs. I was happy to sign for anybody; you didn't worry about whether they were getting your autographs so they could sell them, because the memorabilia market wasn't very big yet. The kids just wanted to have an autographed ball they could display on their bedroom shelf. But Thurman would only sign for the kids who were not so fortunate; if he saw a kid in a wheelchair, he'd stop and talk to him and give him an autograph, and then he'd head straight for the clubhouse.

Usually, the Yankees' PR people didn't even bother to ask Thurman to come out and say hello to visiting groups before the game, because they knew he'd say, "Get outta here!" But if there was a veterans group in attendance, or some kids with cerebral palsy or other issues, Thurman would be the first one to go over and say hey and give them some autographed balls. He would do that instinctively; you didn't have to tell or ask him to do it. But no way for anybody else. Because before the ballgame, the main thing he was always thinking about was, "We've gotta win this game!"

Thurman was a tremendously skilled catcher, of course, but watching him in action in '71, I realized that he was tremendously crafty as well. He wasn't just a guy who could call a great game, he was also a real manipulator and maneuverer, a guy who could find an advantage in any situation. He would talk to every batter who came up, say things like, "You better get ready to swing—the ball is going to be on that top part of the plate," or "The ball is going to be inside." Not too many catchers would do that; whenever I used to get up to bat, they might ask me, "How you doin'?" and stuff like that, but I never knew a catcher to ever say anything to me beyond that, except maybe Bill Freehan of the Tigers, because I would sometimes hit his head with my backswing, which he didn't appreciate.

But Thurman really knew how to push guys' buttons and take their mind off of what they were supposed to be doing. They'd be wondering if Thurman was kidding or telling them the truth, and that was just enough distraction to put them at a disadvantage. And Thurman always knew that if a guy looked bad swinging at the last pitch his last time up, he would be looking for the same pitch on the next one. Thurman might say to him, "Here comes that same pitch that you can't seem to hit," and then he would call for a completely different pitch, just to totally screw up his mind. Or he'd say, "This isn't going to be a good fastball," but it *becomes* a good fastball because they're thinking it's going to be a curveball.

Through the years we played together, I saw him get under the skin of so many great hitters, like Al Kaline, Frank Robinson, and Dick Allen. Allen especially hated how Thurman would mess with him between pitches. He was a guy who could hit the ball harder than anybody, but he hated to bat when Thurman was catching. Thurman would tell him, "We're throwing you a fastball," and he'd think a breaking pitch was coming; but then it would be a fastball just like he said, and that would totally screw him up.

Thurman was such a character back there. But no batter ever turned around and told him to shut up, because he'd already gained everyone's respect as a catcher. They might not have liked him or liked how he played, but they respected him. They knew he was at the top of the game, and they respected that.

Thurman's major thing was always getting the pitcher to win that ballgame. It didn't matter if it was the ace of the staff or an untested rookie; he always wanted to make the pitcher the best pitcher he could be. That always excited Thurman, being a catcher who got the most out of his pitchers. And one of the ways he helped them out was to scuff the ball for them.

Nowadays, if you get one little grass stain on the ball, they immediately throw it out. But the pitchers back then, they *wanted* the scuffed balls. A good pitcher will find that place on the ball and use it to their advantage. Because if you throw a ball at 90 to 100 miles an hour and it's scuffed, you can make it move in a variety of ways that last two inches before it gets to home plate, and that increases the chances that the hitter will pop it up or hit a ground ball. And if it's a situation where there's a couple of guys on base, you definitely want to increase your chance of getting that grounder or pop fly.

Back when we were playing, the batter's boxes weren't as well-groomed as they are now. They'd be filled with gravel and little pebbles, and if a batter kicked the dirt around in the box, those little rocks would go all over the place. Thurman would always stash some of that gravel in the back pocket of his uniform pants. A lot of guys put their chewing tobacco or bubblegum back there, but Thurman had gravel in it. In a key situation, he would reach back into his pocket with his right hand and bring a little gravel out and use it to scuff the ball a bit before throwing it back to the pitcher. Mel Stottlemyre threw a great sinker, and it would move even more when Thurman scuffed the ball up for him.

The American League umpires still used those big chest protectors back then that were like shields. They'd let it go every time they'd call a ball or strike, and then they'd have to pull it back up into position before the next pitch. And Thurman knew that whenever they'd pull it up, he had a second where he could scuff the ball without them noticing. It's all about the timing, and Thurman had that timing down. Sometimes Thurman would roll the ball back to the mound after a pitcher struck somebody out with a scuffed ball; and if it was a strike three to end the inning, Thurman would take that ball back to the dugout with him, because he knew the pitcher could use it again for the first pitch the next inning. If a batter asked the umpire to look at the ball and see if it was scuffed, Thurman would just throw it out himself—roll it or throw it over to the ball boy to put in the bag for batting practice. He'd get rid of it real quick.

Thurman was also great at handling pitchers from a psychological standpoint. If one of our guys started to get wild, or he'd struggle and give up a couple of home runs, Thurman was always great about going out to the mound to calm him down. He might say something funny or give him a good ribbing, but it would get him to laugh and take his mind off everything for a second and relax. He wouldn't necessarily even talk about the game; he'd say something to make the guy laugh, forget about his struggles for a second, and by the time he threw his next pitch it was a brand-new ballgame. Thurman was a genius like that. And that was one of the many reasons he was so great to have on the team.

I also never, ever saw him back down or shy away from a collision at the plate, whether he was running or catching. Back then, you *had* to run into the catcher; even if he was already holding the ball, you had try and knock it out of his glove. If you didn't, your teammates would jump down your throat, the press would write about it in the papers, and your manager might not play you the next day. Even if you break your arm, you've gotta run into the catcher. I remember having some big collisions at the plate with Bill Freehan, and he was a really big, tough guy.

Thurman knew that every runner coming home was going to try and knock him down; it was part of his job description. It didn't matter if it was a big guy like Gates Brown, Willie Horton, Frank Howard, or Boog Powell, he was ready for it. You could knock him 15 feet off the plate, and he'd just get up, put his mask back on, and get ready for the next pitch. When he'd come back to the dugout, you might hear him grunt when he sat down, and you'd know he was hurting, but he would never show it on the field.

Thurman continued to struggle at the plate for the rest of the 1971 season; his batting average (.251) and OBP (.335) both finished exactly 51 points below his 1970 marks. He was outstanding defensively, and nailed a league-leading 61 percent of the runners who tried to steal against him. Though deserving of the Gold Glove Award, he lost out to Ray Fosse of the Cleveland Indians.

Ron's half-season with the 1971 Yankees was a stellar one. Playing almost entirely against right-handed pitchers, he hit .322 in 199 at-bats, with seven home runs, 31 RBIs, and a .363 OBP. Nicknamed "Boomer" by Yankees announcer Phil Rizzuto for the prodigious home runs he'd hit in batting practice, Ron quickly became a favorite with the fans and the press thanks to his garrulous personality.

The 1971 Yankees never managed to get more than five games over .500, and they would finish in fourth place in the AL East with an 82–80 mark, a distant 21 games behind the first-place Orioles. They finished the season in an unintentionally memorable fashion, earning a forfeit victory against the Washington Senators when D.C. fans—angry that Senators owner Bob Short was moving the franchise to Texas—poured onto the field at RFK Stadium in the ninth inning and began tearing up the place.

I missed all the craziness in D.C. because I'd already left the team so I could spend Yom Kippur with my wife, and then I had to do two weeks of military duty in Syracuse. But Thurman told me that Frank Howard hit one of the longest homers he ever saw. He said things started getting crazy with the fans around the fifth inning, and then everybody ran out on the field in the ninth. "Bloomie, we got outta there pretty quickly," he laughed when he told me about it. We were actually losing at the time all those Senators fans tore up the field, so we would have finished 81–81 if they hadn't won the game for us like that.

Mike Kekich pitched for us in that game, and I always figured that the fans were probably so upset because every start of his was like 16 hours long. Kekich would go 3-2 on every hitter, and Thurman used to get so frustrated with him—he'd start off 0-2 on a batter, and you knew it was going to be 3-2 before he got the guy out. He always seemed to be the guy we'd have pitching on the last game of a road trip, and he was not the guy you wanted to have pitching when you just wanted to go home.

Kekich was like Thurman's pet project—Thurman would always try to get him into a steady rhythm, but Mike's idea of a steady rhythm was going 3-2 on every hitter. And he would shake Thurman off all the time, and they would have these heated confrontations on the mound about it. Thurman was aggressive, and if you're not aggressive out on that mound, it's business to him—he wants to win that ballgame. Pitchers are not going to have a good game every time out, and Thurman knew that, but the bottom line was, if you don't listen to

Thurman and you get knocked around, then Thurman doesn't have any respect for you. He would jump down Mike's throat all the time, because Mike was a left-hander who had real good stuff, but he would never listen to Thurman and he would get hit around because of it. He had a great arm but a two-cent head.

Thurman went back to Canton for the off-season, and I stayed in New York. I used to go over to Yankee Stadium and hang out in the clubhouse and talk with Pete Sheehy, the equipment manager. The old Yankee clubhouse was all brick walls and metal lockers, and Pete had this massive mahogany desk in there. It was like 150 years old, and big enough for like 10 or 12 people to sit around it. And everybody who had played for the Yankees had carved their names into the desk, people like Babe Ruth, Lou Gehrig, Joe DiMaggio, and Mickey Mantle.

During the season, Pete Sheehy would always be sitting there doing something. Back then, if you were missing a button on your uniform, they wouldn't send it out to a seamstress to be replaced. Pete Sheehy would always put the button on, while sitting at his desk. We used to come in before the game, and he'd have like four-dozen balls sitting on his desk, which he'd ask all the players to sign. The first thing he'd say to you when you came in was, "Bloomie, you need to sign the balls."

"Okay, Pete, I will!"

"Thurman, I've got four-dozen balls you need to sign!"

"Okay, Pete."

Thurman hated signing those balls, though. Even I hated signing the balls! It's one thing to sign an autograph here and there, but the last thing you want to do before a ballgame is get a cramp in your hand from signing your name almost 50 times in a row.

Pete knew that Thurman hated to sign the balls, and he'd wind up signing them himself. That's why it's so hard to find a Yankees team ball with a genuine Thurman Munson autograph. Pete Sheehy was the best forger—he could write an autograph of Mickey Mantle, Whitey Ford, or Yogi Berra that was absolutely perfect. He could sign my autograph exactly like I'd written it. And those four-dozen balls would be gone at the end of the night, whether or not we'd actually signed them. I think probably 90 percent of the Thurman signatures out there on Yankee team balls are actually Pete's.

The clubhouse was Pete's home, and I loved sitting with him there. When it was quiet and nobody was around, he would tell me stories about all the great ballplayers he'd worked with. He'd seen everything; he could have written the greatest book if he'd ever wanted to. I'm a rookie, a kid, and he's telling me about Babe Ruth and Lou Gehrig, and how they'd joke around with one another. He'd tell me about Ryne Duren, all those guys.

One day we were talking, and I said, "What do you think about Thurman?"

And he said, "He reminds me a lot of Bill Dickey—his body type, how he looks, how he moves. Thurman's going to be a great one. You watch." Pete knew, right off the bat.

5

Where Were You in '72?

It was an unseasonably hot March night in Fort Lauderdale, and we were playing a spring training exhibition game at Little Yankee Stadium. I can't remember who we were playing, but I remember I wasn't in the lineup that night.

I was sitting on the dugout bench with Rich McKinney and Jerry Kenney, and I'll be honest: We weren't paying attention to the game. We were joking around, checking out some of the women up in the stands—who we liked, who we didn't like. Like I said, it was pretty hot out for March, and the women at the game were dressed accordingly, which we didn't mind at all.

McKinney was a real cutup. The Yankees had gotten him from the White Sox over the winter in exchange for Stan Bahnsen, and he was supposed to be our new starting third baseman. But I thought it was kind of a bad sign when he showed up for the first day of spring training and immediately

73

made a beeline for our trainer, Joe Soares. The first thing out of his mouth to Joe was, "What do you do for crabs?"

"What do you mean, what do I do for them?" Joe asked.

"I got the crabs!" Rich told him, his voice a panicked whisper. "I been out all night long, and I'm messed up!" And this was his first day with the ballclub!

We called McKinney "Crabs" from then on, and we also called him "Bozo," because his hair was big and fuzzy and red—it was almost as big as the Afro that Oscar Gamble used to have. "Bozo" also made sense as a nickname for him, because he had no idea where he was half the time; if you'd put his brain in a bird, it would have flown backwards. I swear he'd show up to games sometimes without his glove, and he'd always lose track of his bat. Most of the time, he seemed to be much more interested in talking about women than talking about—or playing—baseball.

But Bozo was hilarious, and boy could he make us laugh. Which is what Jerry and I were doing with him during that night game in Fort Lauderdale, when Thurman suddenly appeared in front of us, steaming mad. He was in a grumpy mood to begin with—I think he was having a bad game at the plate, or somebody'd fouled a ball off his foot—and now he was looking like he was ready to kill someone. He walked over to the dugout water fountain, which was one of those old ones like we used to have in the school hallway, where you press the button on the spout and the water comes up. With a single motion, he grabbed it, ripped it from its base and threw it to the ground next to where we were sitting. And then, now that he had our undivided attention, he completely unloaded on us.

"When I'm playing the game, don't you *ever* make a joke about it," he raged, while water from the busted fountain spurted out all over the dugout. "You *watch* the game! Do you understand?" No one said anything. We just sat there, petrified. Thurman paused for a second, took a deep breath, and looked directly at me.

"Bloomie, you're gonna be facing this guy this season," he said, pointing out at whoever was pitching against us at that moment. "You've gotta watch him *now* and learn what he does, so you know what to expect when you come up against him!" Thurman's lecture would have gone on, but we had to vacate the dugout—the busted plumbing was dumping so much water onto the floor that it was already coming up to our ankles. The Yankees had to call an engineer down to the dugout to fix it that night, because Thurman had completely broken the pipe the fountain had been attached to. We spent the rest of the game on the grass, drying out in foul territory.

After the ballgame was over, I went up to Thurman in the clubhouse. He was still in a foul mood, and I knew it wasn't always a good idea to try and talk to him when he was feeling that way, but I felt like I had to say something. "Look, Thurmie," I told him, "I made a mistake, and I apologize." He grunted and didn't look up. I turned and started walking away.

"Hey, I'm only saying this for your own good," he called out from behind me. "You're gonna wind up facing this guy in the ninth inning sometime, and you've gotta know how he's gonna throw, because we're gonna need you to get a base hit off him and win the ballgame."

My first impulse was to say to Thurman, "I *was* watching him; I was just joking around with the guys while I was doing it." But I knew he'd know that was BS, and Thurman never had much use for excuses. So I just told him, "Okay, you're right. It won't happen again."

That was the first time he ever really got on to me like that. But from then on, he would always remind me, "Watch the game. I want to get a ring on my finger, and I want to get a ring with the New York Yankees, and I want you to be part of it." I wanted that, too.

Thurman got on McKinney an awful lot after that, too, but McKinney didn't care. It was like he was on another planet. He didn't do too much for our team, unfortunately, and he didn't even show up to the ballpark sometimes. He wound up getting sent down to the minors at the end of May. Stan Bahnsen, on the other hand, won 21 games for the White Sox in 1972. That wasn't a good trade.

"*Strike" was the big buzzword of Spring Training '72, and not because everyone was swinging and missing. For the first time in history, MLB players—led by Marvin Miller, the executive director of the Major League Baseball Players Association— were preparing for a work stoppage. The three-year pension agreement between MLB players and team owners was set to expire at the end of March, and the players were requesting that the owners increase the amount of their contribution to the pension fund in accordance with recent inflation. It was a modest request, all things considered; but instead of honoring it, the staunchly anti-labor owners flatly refused, believing that new pension negotiations offered the perfect opportunity to smash the players' union, which they viewed as at best unnecessary and at worst a serious threat.*

As the showdown with the owners loomed ever closer, Miller spent much of March visiting the various teams' spring training facilities to educate the players on what was happening with the pension agreement, and to gauge their willingness to walk out if their demands weren't met. Instead of folding, as the owners fully expected them to, the players surprised even Miller with their resolve to fight; on March 31, less than a week before Opening Day, the 48 players union reps voted 47–0 in favor of a strike, with one abstention.

Marvin Miller came to spring training and told us that it was very likely that ownership was not going to give in to our demands, and the only way for us to fight back was to strike.

We had no idea what it would mean; even Jack Aker and Fritz Peterson, our player representatives, weren't sure. At first, we thought we were going to strike and still get our salary, which shows you how little we knew about labor relations. We asked Marvin, "Are we going to get paid?"

"No," he told us.

"Well then, how are we gonna survive? How are we going to get back to New York? How are we going to pay our rent?"

We're down in spring training, and we're not getting paid our salaries yet; the Yankees are paying for our hotel and giving us a few dollars a day for meal money, but that's all. The Players Association didn't have any money in reserve for if we went on strike, we were just gonna have to do without. And we all had bills to pay—I remember I owed like $200 to American Express and other places. Thurman asked Marvin, "How are we going to do this?"

And Marvin, like he always did, said, "It's going to work out, but you've gotta give up something to get something."

None of us really understood the economics of the situation. All the owners claimed they had no money, but we couldn't get into their books to see if that was true. We were all playing on one-year contracts back then, for not a lot of money. If we played well one season, we could ask for a raise for the next one—but the team didn't have to give you a raise, and if they did it would probably be a small one. In fact, they could even *cut* your salary if you didn't play as well as you did the season before.

They gave us what they wanted to back then. It was basically, "Take it or leave it—and if you don't sign, we'll get somebody from Triple A who *wants* to be up in the big leagues." And then, if they send you down to the minor leagues, there's a 75 percent chance you don't get called back up to the Yankees—either you stay down in the minors forever, like so many of those guys I played with at Syracuse, or they trade you as a spare part to another team. You just didn't want to put yourself in that position as an individual player. But Marvin Miller told us that, if we all stood up together, they couldn't send us *all* down to the minors.

After camp broke, Thurman and I and our wives got rooms at the Holiday Inn in Paramus, New Jersey, right over the George Washington Bridge from New York City. We were both in peak spring training shape, and we wanted to stay that way during the strike, so we decided to drive over to Yankee Stadium together and work out. Several other players had the same idea, but we were all shocked when we showed up and were told by security that the field was off-limits to the players as long as the strike was going on. They would let us change in the clubhouse, but that was it; all equipment, and even the showers, was off-limits.

We weren't even allowed to park in the players' parking lot, but the police knew who we were, and let us park our cars over by Macombs Dam Park. The park's public baseball field, which was right across from Yankee Stadium, became our temporary daily workout spot. Roy White, Jerry Kenney,

Gene Michael, Mel Stottlemyre, Fritz Peterson, Horace Clarke, Rich Hinton, and Rusty Torres were some of the guys who joined us. We all got gloves and bats and balls from sporting goods stores or from home, and we'd show up every morning in our shorts and sweatshirts to take batting practice, shag flies, field grounders, and throw the ball around. We weren't playing actual ballgames, but when word got out that we were playing there, all these Yankee fans would show up to watch us work out.

We had no idea how long the strike would last, and we'd call up Jack Aker every day and ask him, "Did you hear anything?" We would turn on the news radio as soon as we woke up, hoping for an update. Thurman and I enjoyed our daily workouts at Macombs Dam Park, and we often went out to lunch with some of the guys afterwards, which was fun, but we weren't getting paid for it. Plus, we were itching to play ball, for real.

The 1972 strike lasted two weeks. The owners, who'd belatedly realized that they were losing more money from canceled games than it would have cost them to give in to the Players Association's original demands, agreed to increase the pension fund by $500,000. It was also agreed, however, that the 86 scheduled games from the first two weeks of the season would not be made up, which meant that the players would not be *paid for them. Since the teams had anywhere from 153 to 156 games remaining on their schedules, it was decided that the division races would be decided strictly on the basis of winning percentage.*

The work stoppage provoked an extremely negative response from baseball fans and writers alike, many of whom sided fully with the team owners. The general consensus was that the players were privileged to play baseball for a living, and their "greed" in holding out for a greater pension contribution had nullified the sense of joy and expectation that usually surrounds Opening Day. When the season officially began on April 15, a lot of paying customers stayed away (the Yankees sold only 11,319 tickets for their first home game of the year, down considerably from the 34,745 sold for Opening Day in 1971), and many of those who did show up hurled abuse at their former heroes. But major changes were on their way— specifically, the elimination of the reserve clause that had bound players to their teams in perpetuity, and the subsequent advent of full-scale free agency—and these would not have come to pass without Miller and the players leveraging their labor in 1972.

When Marvin finally came back to us and told us that we won, we were happy that we could start playing again, but it didn't really feel like a "win" to us at the time. Our paychecks weren't any higher, and in fact we were going to be making less for the season, because we weren't going to be paid for our "time off." But Marvin assured us that, down the line, what we'd done was going to be for everyone's benefit. We still didn't know about free agency, or how long you'd have to be with your team to qualify for it—all that would come a few years later. We didn't know that a time would soon come when multi-year contracts would be standard, or that players would ever make that much more money than we were making in '72, but Marvin knew.

Some of the players now, they haven't heard of Marvin Miller, they have no idea who he is. And I look at them and think, "If it wasn't for Marvin Miller, you'd be getting seven dollars a day for meal money. You'd be like us, making $15,000 a year, or whatever that would be in today's money, instead of making $4 million a year." They don't understand how we got here. Marvin was finally inducted into the Hall of Fame in 2020; I can't believe it took so long for him to get in there. What he did for us was incredible.

The Yankees didn't spend a day of the 1972 season in first place. But despite their rather lackluster-looking final record of 79–76, they remained very much "in the hunt" in the intensely competitive AL East until the final week, when five consecutive losses relegated them to fourth place, 6.5 games behind the division-winning Detroit Tigers.

That Tigers team was tough. They had great pitching, especially Mickey Lolich and Joe Coleman; they had great older players like Al Kaline, Jim Northrup, Norm Cash, and Willie Horton; and they had an unbelievable young third baseman named Aurelio Rodriguez, who had the best arm at third that I've ever seen—his throws were like laser beams. Billy Martin was their manager that year, and he really had them firing on all cylinders.

Even though Tiger Stadium was old, it was absolutely beautiful, and it was one of our favorite places to play. It was a great park to hit in; it was so intimate, you could actually talk to fans in the stands during the game, and we always drew a lot of Yankee fans whenever we'd play there. Even though the dugouts were small and the clubhouse was hot, the field was always beautifully manicured, and you could tell that the place had some real history to it, just like Yankee Stadium or Fenway Park.

Whenever we'd play in Detroit, we'd always stay at the Hotel Cadillac, which was only about a mile from the ballpark. If the weather was nice, Thurman and I would often walk over to the park together, and sometimes we'd walk back to the hotel, too. It wasn't the nicest walk, but we didn't want to just hang around the hotel, and there wasn't much else to do in downtown Detroit. Sometimes after the game, we'd go to Carl's Chop House or over to Greektown, or we'd go to the Lindell AC, which was this grungy bar where Billy Martin and some of the Tigers players would hang out. It wasn't unusual for us to socialize with players from other teams after games, especially if we were on a road trip, and we'd hang out with Norm Cash at the Lindell AC all the time. He was a crazy guy; whenever you got to first base against the Tigers, you had to be careful about how you got back to the bag on a pickoff throw, because Norm would always put his body between you and the bag, and hit you right in the nuts with his glove. He'd always be yelling hilarious things at us during batting practice, trying to get us to crack up while we were swinging. That always annoyed Thurman, because he always tried to be completely tuned in whenever he was taking BP. If we tried to joke around with him while he was in the cage, he wouldn't even look at us.

Willie Horton opened his restaurant and bar, Club 23, in Detroit in '72, and Thurman and I used to go there a lot. The first time we went there, we tried to walk straight from the ballpark, which was a bad idea. We had to go through several pretty rough neighborhoods, and we got lost a couple of times on the way. Nobody messed with us, though, and Willie was overjoyed to see us when we finally showed up. Thurman and Willie always got along well; Willie was just a real sweetheart. Out on the field, he was a tough guy; but when you'd see him out after the game, he was a great guy to talk to. Gates Brown, too; that guy always killed us, but if you saw him at the bar afterward he was a lot of fun and always nice as could be.

Shortly before the end of spring training, the Yankees traded first baseman Danny Cater to the Boston Red Sox in exchange for a relief pitcher named Sparky Lyle. The trade has since gone down as one of the most infamously lopsided in Red Sox history—Lyle led the AL with 35 saves in '72, and was a major factor in the Yankees' competitive showing, while Cater hit only .237 for Boston, who might have actually won the AL East if they'd still had a reliable closer. But the trade was also a boon for Ron, since it cleared the way for him to play first base, at least against right-handed starting pitchers.

I played first base in '72, and it was so much fun, because I had such a great view of Thurman. I loved watching him catch. He was *pretty* to watch, if that makes sense.

Whenever I was playing first base, Thurman would spit to alert me that there was a pickoff on. If there's a man on first base with a big lead and I'm behind him, Thurman would turn his head to the right and spit, and that meant I should expect a pitchout or a snap throw down to first. A lot of catchers in that situation would kick their right foot as the signal, or put their hand on their right leg, but you'd be able to pick that up if you watched them for a while. Thurman would simply spit, like ballplayers do all the time, but that was a great signal for me because I knew that Thurman never chewed tobacco—I don't think he even chewed sunflower seeds—so if he spit there was a reason behind it. But people never picked up on that.

Thurman was always aware that other players and coaches might be trying to steal his signs, so he would change things up all the time. Sometimes he would intentionally drop the ball after catching it, which was a signal to be alert for the throw down to first. Thurman was so quick with his hands, it was the most amazing thing you've ever seen. It was like watching Rod Carew play second; the ball would barely touch his mitt and he'd already thrown it. Thurman wasn't smooth like Carew; he was herky-jerky out on the field. But he could get that ball out of his mitt as fast as anybody. He'd throw sidearm or even underhanded, and that's why his ball tailed. But he was so good at it, it was hard to get a good jump on him.

A lot of the big base-stealers who played against us back then were fast, but they weren't quick with getting a jump— they would steal on the pitcher, in other words. We had some pitchers like Fred Beene and Mel Stottlemyre, who had quick motions, but we also had guys like Sparky Lyle, who definitely took their time up there, so Thurman's quick release was key in preventing players from stealing. There would be times where Thurman would intentionally drop the pitch and make it look like it was getting past him, just to deke the guy on first. The guy would see that and take off, and then Thurman would snatch up the ball and whip it to second for the out. It was a beautiful thing to watch.

Thurman was like a computer. He knew which guys would run on the first pitch after being looked back to first by the pitcher, and which guys wouldn't. He knew who was quick, too, like Bert Campaneris of the A's. Bert wasn't fast, but he was quick as lightning. He would just shoot past you like that, and he had a lot of steals. But he only rarely tried to run on Thurman, because he knew how quick Thurman's hands were.

Thurman also made good use of those quick hands when it came to playing pranks. The first time we went down to Texas to play the Rangers, I bought a cowboy hat, a big Stetson, that I paid like $15 for. I bought it in the morning of the last game of the series. After the game, we were going straight to the airport to fly somewhere else, so I wore my hat on the bus from the hotel to the ballpark. I was so proud of that hat. Nobody said anything about it on the bus, but I knew there were guys on the team who were serious instigators, guys like Fritz Peterson and Mike Kekich who would do anything to irritate anybody. So when we got to the clubhouse, I hid that hat behind my clothes while nobody was looking. After the game was over, I pulled the hat out, and it was covered with everybody's signatures; Thurman had snuck it out, got everyone to sign it, and stashed it back in its hiding place.

I didn't learn my lesson. The next time we went to Texas, I bought *another* cowboy hat and took it on the bus with me, completely forgetting what they'd done to my other one. I hid it again, but as I was stepping up to the plate to take batting practice, I looked out at the flagpole and saw something flapping in the breeze. It was my new hat. In just a few minutes, Thurman and Fritz and Stottlemyre had somehow taken it, drilled a hole in it, and sent it up the ballpark flagpole, right under the flag. So I knew never to do that again, but I was so upset because the $15 or $20 that I paid for it was a heck of a lot of money back then!

We all loved Phil Rizzuto. He was great, but he was crazy; he was quirky. He always had to have his Diet Coke with cherry juice in it. And he hated bugs. Whenever the Yankees were presenting an award or a present to somebody before a game, they'd put a microphone out at home plate, and Phil would make the announcement. And whenever this would happen, Thurman and the gang would leave something like a dead praying mantis on the microphone, or go down into the "dungeons" of Yankee Stadium and find a dead rat to put on the mic. Rizzuto would walk over to the mic, and see the dead bug or rat on it, and he would just go nuts. He would drop the mic and storm off the field and not come back, and the people from whatever association was there to be honored would be left standing there, wondering what the heck was going on.

Thurman and Ron both put up solid numbers in 1972. Thurman raised his batting average to .280, while starting 132 games behind the plate. And while Ron's average dropped to .268, his 14 home runs were the second-most on the team behind Bobby Murcer's 33. But the thrill of playing together in their first real pennant race aside, one of the most momentous things that happened to Thurman and Ron in 1972 was the blossoming of their friendship with Nat Tarnopol.

Tarnopol was a tall, good-looking, and charismatic Jewish guy from Detroit who'd been a star shortstop in high school, but—despite contract offers from the Tigers and the White Sox—decided to make his fortune in the world of R&B music instead. He was instrumental in the success of soul singer Jackie Wilson, as well as other 1950s and '60s soul and R&B acts, and by the time Thurman and Ron met him, he'd already worked his way up to the presidency of Brunswick Records. A diehard Yankee fan and season-ticketholder, Tarnopol was already friendly with several players and coaches on the team, but he took a special liking to Ron. Growing up a fan of the Tigers' legendary Jewish slugger Hank Greenberg, Tarnopol was well aware of all the anti-Semitism that Greenberg had faced, and he took it upon himself to ensure that Ron felt at home in New York City.

Seventeen years older than Ron, Tarnopol became something of a surrogate father to him, and grew extremely close to Thurman, as well. But the fact that two of their star players were palling around with a flamboyant player from the music business—a sketchy world with no shortage of mob involvement—made the staid, CBS-owned Yankees extremely uncomfortable.

There was a part of Nat that always wished he'd been a ballplayer. So when I came up with the Yankees as this Jewish novelty, I think he saw something of himself in me. In '71, he'd tried to get the Yankees to do a "Ron Blomberg Day" before I'd even been with the team for a couple of weeks. It didn't happen, but that's the kind of guy he was.

In '72, I was looking for a place to live, since my wife and I didn't want to stay out in Paramus anymore. Nat said, "Come on, we need to find you a place to live," so we went up to Riverdale, this heavily Jewish neighborhood in the Bronx, driving in Nat's Rolls-Royce. We pulled up at this place called the Whitehall Building, up on 232nd Street and Henry Hudson Parkway. It was absolutely gorgeous; it had a doorman, chandeliers in the lobby, tennis courts, a big swimming pool, everything, and it overlooked the Hudson River.

Nat and I walked into the building's management office and he told them, "I need a two-bedroom apartment." They showed us one, it was absolutely gorgeous, and he said, "We'll take it!"

I said, "Nat, I don't have the money to pay for this!"

He said, "What are you worried about?"

"I don't have the money to pay for the furniture and the carpet and the drapes, much less this apartment."

"It's taken care of," he said. "Give me about four or five days, and you're gonna move in!"

I go up there about a week later, and I've got shag carpeting—which was real big at the time—TVs in every room, everything was painted, I had new appliances and furniture, and everything was gorgeous. He'd gotten some teamsters to move everything in and fix up the place. I was only making $16,000 a year, but now I had this great place in Riverdale. Willie Mays was my "upstairs neighbor"—he lived up in the penthouse, and I lived on the second floor. I ran into him by the elevators and introduced myself, and I wound up going to lunch with him at one of the delis in the neighborhood, which was a real thrill.

I was still driving my old Oldsmobile Toronado at the time, and Nat thought that just wouldn't do. He knew the people at this Cadillac place called Potamkin, who were always happy to do him a favor, and he told me to go down there and get an Eldorado. Those cars were as big as a bus, so I told him, "No way—who's gonna park this thing?" Two weeks later, he picked me up at my place and took me to Pepe Motors out in White Plains. I just thought we were going up there to have lunch with his friend, the old guy who owned the place. But we get to the showroom, and Nat pointed to a new Mercedes 450SL and said, "Why don't you get into that car?" I got in, and he asked me, "What do you think?"

"I love this car! It's gorgeous!"

He said, "It's yours!"

"Nat," I said, "I've already got a car at the house!"

He goes, "Nah, we're gonna get somebody to bring it up here for you."

He paid cash for it. It was this gorgeous silver convertible, which I think cost about $13,000 back then, which was almost my entire salary. Nat knew a guy who put pinstripes on it for me, which I didn't even know was possible. When I pulled up to the Yankee Stadium parking lot in it for the first time, Thurman's eyes just about bugged out. "Where did you get *that*?" he said. Three weeks later, Nat bought a 450SL for Thurman, as well. Some of the guys on the team were a little jealous about that, because nobody was driving cars that nice back then. Thurman wasn't a flashy guy, but boy did he love that Mercedes!

Nat and I really connected because of the Jewish thing, but he and Thurman's bond was definitely business-related. Thurman was already buying property back in Canton, and he was fascinated by the world of real estate and finance. If you gave Thurman a newspaper, he'd turn to the stocks report before he'd even think of looking at the sports pages. And through Nat, Thurman met a lot of heavy hitters in that world, people who owned high-rise office buildings and banks and were all too happy to let the Yankees' star catcher pick their brains about making investments.

Nat knew some other kinds of heavy hitters, as well. There was one guy who was almost always with him, Carmine "Wassel" DeNoia. He was 6'4", 250 pounds, and he *looked* like a Wassel, whatever that was. He was very nice to us, but he could be very intimidating. So could these other guys Nat liked to hang with: a tough guy named Johnny Roberts and a big Black guy named Gerald Sims—or just "Sims," as everybody called him. I was really naïve about these guys, to be honest; I didn't even realize until years later that they were gangsters. To me, gangsters were supposed to look like Al Capone and the guys on that TV show *The Untouchables*. But they were big-hearted guys who treated Thurman and I like we were their long-lost brothers, and they'd do anything for us.

We would often go down and hang out at Nat's office at 888 7th Avenue, up on one of the top floors of this big glass-and-steel building. Wassel, Sims, and Johnny Roberts would usually be there, and sometimes Roy White and Jerry Kenney and Elston Howard, who were all friends with Nat, would join us. We would go out to lunch at the Stage Deli, or Nat would have a Chinese place nearby send up a bunch of food. Sometimes we would all go to this barbershop around the corner from Nat's office and get haircuts and shaves, and Nat would know everybody who came in there. It was all Italian guys, with the gold chains and big rings on their hands, and we'd talk baseball.

Nat always dressed extremely well. Thurman and I used to make fun of him, because he was always wearing suede shoes and a suede jacket wherever he went. He was very generous, and people liked him. He wasn't the type of guy who held on to every penny he made; he was the type of guy who was always giving. I think his family went through some hard times while he was growing up, so he wanted to help other people. Everywhere we'd go, he'd always tip the staff extremely well, and they always took care of him. Nat was never one to do the "Don't you know who I am?" kind of thing. At that time, Nat could have gotten anything he wanted in New York, or hung out with anyone he wanted to. But he loved to hang out with us and hear our stories—hear about things that happened on the road, or pranks we used to play on other players.

Nat never talked about the dark side of the record business to us; it was always about which of his records were on the *Billboard* charts, which of his artists were coming through on tour, that kind of stuff. He had gold records all over his office walls. People were constantly coming and going from Nat's office. We met a lot of Brunswick recording artists—people like The Chi-Lites, Tyrone Davis, and Hamilton Bohannon—and a lot of shady-looking guys who were always coming in with boxes and big briefcases. If there was any real business to be discussed, like with Johnny Roberts (who turned out to be Jackie Wilson's manager) or another visitor, Nat would excuse himself from our conversation and go into a different room with the guy, or we'd clear out of the office for a bit. One time, he called me in after some guy had just left, and he said, "I got watches for you and your wife." He had a whole box full of expensive watches on his desk, and he pulled two brand new Piaget diamond watches out of it and handed them to me. I don't think I ever wore mine, but that was typical of Nat's generosity. Of course, I never knew where those watches came from, or why these people were giving them to him.

Nat would come to just about every game we played at Yankee Stadium, and sit right behind our dugout. He would bring people from the music business—Clive Davis, Motown people, his own acts from his label, and, of course, Wassel and Sims—and Thurman and I would stand at the railing and talk to them before the game. Sometimes Nat even came out onto the field to talk to us, and security wouldn't say a thing about it, because all those guys knew Nat too. After the game, Nat would often take us out to eat at Manero's, which was a legendary steakhouse in Greenwich, Connecticut. Nat would make a phone call to the restaurant from the stadium, telling them that we were on our way up there, and they'd have a table all ready for us by the time we got up there. They had an incredible chopped salad, and their french fries, and the steaks—this place was just incredible. That was Thurman's favorite place, too; he called it "the greatest steakhouse in the world."

Sometimes, if we were running late after a game, Nat would call ahead to Manero's and they would stay open just for us; we'd bring 'em a signed baseball to say thanks. And like at the Stage Deli, the owner wouldn't let us order. There would just be this endless parade of steaks, ribs, salads, desserts, everything—it just kept on coming! We had our own little room in there, and we'd just sit there, talking baseball and eating until two in the morning. We were so used to eating late, because after a night game on a road trip we normally wouldn't eat until almost midnight.

Sometimes we'd go with Nat to the Friars Club for dinner; we saw Sammy Davis Jr. there a few times. We met a lot of people there that Nat knew from the record business. That's when I learned how many Jews there were in the record business! One of Nat's best friends was James Nederlander, and he would always get us tickets to Broadway shows, and get us backstage to meet the actors. One time, Thurman and I and our wives went to see *Fiddler on the Roof*, and we went back afterward and met Zero Mostel! It was incredible. I'm still a kid from the South, and I'm not used to meeting people like Zero Mostel or Sammy Davis Jr. or Jack Paar or Tom Snyder or David Carradine or Henny Youngman—all of whom we met through Nat or his connections—much less having them know who I am! All these people that Thurman and I would see on Johnny Carson, and they all knew who we were! We were living the dream!

Hanging with Nat really was like a fantasy for me and Thurman. I mean, I was already living in this incredible apartment, and if I told Nat I needed a TV, there would be two TVs shipped up to me the next day; if I needed a stereo, he'd have Mitsubishi send me a state-of-the-art one that weighed like 400 pounds, and someone would bring it up and put it together for me. And Nat would always make sure that Thurman and I had all the latest cassettes from his artists.

Nat would get us third-row seats at Madison Square Garden to see The Temptations or Gladys Knight and the Pips. Or we'd go to the Apollo Theater in Harlem; the crowds were at least 95 percent black, but they took great care of us. Nat would park his Rolls-Royce right in front of the Apollo, and the ushers would wave us in the front door ahead of all the people in line. It was incredible. We didn't look at ourselves as celebrities; Thurman especially, he wasn't a guy who wanted to go out and get all the attention. Thurman's from Canton, I'm from Atlanta, and we were used to pulling up in pickup trucks, not a Rolls-Royce. We'd never seen any of this kind of stuff. But Thurman was always polite to everybody who'd come up to talk to us.

Thurman didn't understand Nat's kind of music at first, because it wasn't what he'd grown up listening to. Me, I'd gone to see James Brown and Otis Redding several times when I was a kid, and soul and R&B was my favorite music. Thurman was more into stuff like Creedence Clearwater Revival, The Allman Brothers, and The Doobie Brothers. But by getting to know Nat's artists, like Eugene Record of The Chi-Lites, he started getting into soul music as well. When we'd hear The

Chi-Lites' "Oh Girl" or "Have You Seen Her" on the radio, Thurman would smile and say, "Hey, we know that guy!"

Nat and his family had a gorgeous house up in Purchase, New York; the film *Goodbye, Columbus* had been shot there, and it was this huge estate with a swimming pool and a stable and pastures for the horses he and his wife had. Purchase is really built up now, but back then it was really out in the country—but it was also only like a 20-minute drive from Yankee Stadium, and Thurman and I spent a lot of time up there. If we'd play a weekend day game and had the night free, one of us would always ask, "We going to Nat's after this?" And the answer was usually "Yeah!"

Nat would have parties where we'd sit by the pool and eat hamburgers with his friends, people like the comedian Soupy Sales, the great jazz guy Lionel Hampton, or Eugene Record. Nat would pull out a boom box and play us the singles his record company was going to put out, before they were ever played on the radio. He would say, "This one is going to be a hit—and it's going to be on the radio two weeks from now."

Thurman was always so happy and relaxed when we were up at Nat's place. Even though we were hanging out with people who had way more money than we did, and were so much more worldly than we were, he felt like he could be himself up there, and Nat really made him feel like he was part of the family. Thurman would dive into the pool with all his clothes on, just to make Nat's kids laugh, and he'd play catch or horse around with them and with the kids of Nat's other friends; he just loved it. There was no "Grumpy Thurman" when we were hanging out at Nat's; he would be so funny and loose and charming, it was beautiful to see. This was the same guy who'd try to kill you if you were going at it with him in a bench-clearing brawl, but here he was a complete teddy bear.

I think Nat really drew Thurman out, and helped bring him out of his shell and be less introverted. He felt comfortable with Nat, because Nat never put him in any situation where he felt uncomfortable, or felt he had to be anyone other than who he was. And it made him a lot looser in the clubhouse. He would play music in his locker, hang out, and joke around. The writers still triggered him, but from watching the way Nat was with people, he knew how to handle them a little better.

Every restaurant we used to go to, it seemed like Nat had his own table and his own waiter that took care of us. It was the life of Riley! He had a table at 21, which was *the* restaurant in New York at the time. We used to go there all the time with him, and we'd often meet Soupy Sales there. Soupy was a big baseball fan, and he was Jewish, so he and I always had a lot to talk about. One night, we were sitting at 21 with Soupy, and we realized that the actress Suzanne Pleshette from *The Bob Newhart Show* was sitting at the table next to us with her agent and mom and dad. Nat and Soupy knew Suzanne from the showbiz world, so we wound up moving the tables together and making it a big party. And the next thing we knew, Angie Dickinson came in with Burt Bacharach, and they sat down with us. It turned out that they were major baseball fans, so we sat there with these famous actresses and this famous songwriter, all of us talking baseball, and we had such a great time.

Thurman was always so great with the celebrities we'd meet through Nat. He was never starstruck by them, but he also never felt threatened by their presence, like he was worried about them out-shining him. He just was who he was—which, away from the ballpark, was a down-to-earth and funny guy with a twinkle in his eye—and these people loved him for it. I remember at the end of that night at 21, we were leaving the restaurant and Thurman (who'd had a few beers by this point) playfully hopped up on one of those iron jockeys that they have lined up at the entrance. I saw a piece of paper fall out of his old plaid sport coat, and reached down to pick it up for him. It was Burt Bacharach's business card. "He told me to give him a call sometime," Thurman shrugged, like it was no big deal that the guy who wrote "What the World Needs Now Is Love" and so many other hits wanted to pal around with him. Because, to Thurman, it wasn't.

Nat's house became our home away from home. In the coming years, Thurman would usually stay there for a week or two during the off-season, like if he was coming back to New York to play in some of the charity basketball games that I'd organize every winter. One night, we were up at Nat's, with just the three of us—me, him, and Thurman—sitting in his den. Nat said to us, "Here, I wanna show you something. Come with me." He had a vault hidden in his house—I don't think his kids even knew about it—and he opened the door and beckoned us to come in with him. It was like a bank vault, and there were thousands of hundred-dollar bills neatly stacked all over the shelves and filing cases. Our jaws just about hit the floor. We'd never seen that much money in one place before! "This is what I'm going to buy the Yankees with!" Nat told us.

CBS was losing a lot of money on the team, in part because attendance was down in '72, and they let it be known that they were looking to sell. Nat was very serious about wanting to buy the Yankees, and he had big plans for the team. For one thing, he was going to fire Ralph Houk and hire Dick Williams from the A's, an old friend of his, to be the manager. For another, he told me, "You're going to play every day." He wasn't going to let Williams just platoon me against righties like Ralph did. I really liked the sound of that, of course. I thought Ralph was a great manager, and I never criticized him in the press for platooning me, even though the writers would sometimes try to get me to do that. But I was a ballplayer, and playing every day was what I was built to do—plus, ballplayers who played every day made more money than platooned first basemen.

But CBS wouldn't sell to Nat. Baseball owners are, by and large, a conservative bunch, and the CBS people knew enough about the shadier side of Nat's life to realize that the rest of the American League owners would likely oppose and prevent a sale of the team to him. That was the only time I ever saw Nat mad, when he realized that it wasn't going to happen.

In fact, the Yankees had a big talk with me about Nat. The guys who were running the show for CBS—Michael Burke, Johnny Johnson, and Lee MacPhail—called me upstairs to their offices in Yankee Stadium and started asking me questions about him. They told me, "You know, Ron, you need to be real careful with a guy like that." And then they started talking about all the people he knew in the record industry, like it was a bad thing.

I didn't know anything, you understand? Nat was a dear friend of mine and Thurman's, and I had no idea what they meant. And it was very difficult, because we'd gotten very close with him, and here are the Yankees telling me I've gotta be careful around him, and that they didn't want me to hang out with him. I felt caught in the middle. But they'd actually checked up on him and his associates, so they knew more about Nat than I did. And of course, here's Nat coming to the ballpark all the time with Wassel, this big mean-looking guy who looks like he's got bodies stashed somewhere, and like he could be carrying a tommy gun under his overcoat.

I think Thurman was maybe a little less naïve about Nat and his friends than I was. Guys like Wassel reminded him of some of the tough guys he knew from back at Tote's pool hall in Canton; and though it didn't faze him to be around them,

I think he knew that everything wasn't entirely on the up-and-up. But they never talked about what they did around us. There was no, "We're going to murder this guy tomorrow." It was never like that. I had no idea what they were up to. They knew we were good kids, and they kept us out of all of that. They simply loved baseball, and they loved hanging out with guys who played for the Yankees. And we loved hanging out with Nat, so it was all good.

The Yankees were also concerned because people in the music industry had a reputation for doing drugs, and they didn't want us getting involved with any of that. Now, I never drank or smoked, and I never took any drugs, not even marijuana. Thurman liked beer, but he was never into any drugs either, and anyone we knew who did drugs kept it away from us. If Nat or his friends or his recording artists wanted to do something, they respected us enough to go into another room and do it; there was never any invitation or pressure for Thurman or me to do those things with them. We were welcomed into their world, but they respected us as professional athletes and didn't involve us in anything that might get us in trouble or affect our playing careers. Like any Yankee fans, they wanted to see us out on the field, playing the best we could play.

Michael Burke was always great to me. He was a very distinguished-looking guy, very classy, a total gentleman, always in a coat and tie. He was a really nice guy, but he wasn't a motivator. Him and Johnny Johnson and Lee MacPhail, they didn't come down to the field or the clubhouse a whole lot to interact with the players; it was more about business to them. And they might make one or two trades in the off-season, but it was never anything big. They kept the team pretty much the same from year to year.

And that was frustrating for us. Thurman and I would always talk about how we just didn't have enough good arms, whether in our minor league system or in our starting rotation and bullpen. We knew we were a good team, but then we would look at teams like the Orioles or the Tigers or the A's, great teams with really strong pitching, and we knew we couldn't really compete with them. We both wished we had an owner who was willing to spend money to help us win, and we were disappointed when Nat was unable to buy the club— not just because he was our friend, but because we knew he would have been a hands-on type of owner. Nat wanted the Yankees to win, and he had the kind of money to spend that was needed to build a winner.

As it turned out, we would get our wish in 1973—we just didn't know how wild things would get when it actually came true.

6

Almost Cut My Hair

Nineteen seventy-three was a transitional year for the Yankees, in several senses. For one thing, it would be the team's last season in the original "House That Ruth Built." Officially opened in 1923, the ballpark hadn't even reached its 50th birthday before starting to literally fall apart, and millions of dollars in public-funded renovations were needed to shore up its structural issues. It was announced that the team would have to play its 1974 and (probably) 1975 seasons at Shea Stadium while the work went on.

For another, CBS had found someone to take the storied franchise off its hands: Ohio shipping magnate George Steinbrenner, who'd tried and failed the previous year to buy the Cleveland Indians, put a group of investors together, including Yankees president Michael Burke, that forked over a reported $10 million for the Yankees in January 1973. (CBS had bought the team in 1966 for $13.2 million.)

Steinbrenner, a fan of the Yankees since childhood, promised that his investment group would operate as "an absentee ownership," and let Burke run the show. "We're not going to pretend we are something that we aren't," Steinbrenner told the press once the sale of the team was made official. "I'll stick to building ships." It would take just about four months for Steinbrenner to break that promise; Burke resigned his position as club president in late April, due to Steinbrenner's micro-managing and his installment of former Indians general manager Gabe Paul—who'd brought Steinbrenner and Burke together in the first place—all of which Burke saw as a blatant affront to his authority.

The Yankees would pull off some momentous trades under Steinbrenner and Paul in the coming years, but no trade was quite so earth-shaking as the one announced in March 1973 between Yankees hurlers Fritz Peterson and Mike Kekich, who had decided to trade wives. While many married American couples were experimenting with "wife-swapping" and "key parties" in the early 1970s, as the sexual revolution of the 1960s took hold in America's middle-class suburbs, this was no one-night affair; the hurlers, who had been best friends for years, revealed that they were also trading houses, children, and even their family pets. To say that the staid Yankees front office was stunned by the Peterson-Kekich swap would be a considerable understatement, but their teammates were also fairly thrown by it.

In 1973, Thurman and I flew into spring training on the same day—him from Canton, me from New York. We arrived at the airport around the same time, met up with Mel Stottlemyre, and took a car together to Schrafft's Inn, the hotel we were staying at. Thurman and I had both grown moustaches during the off-season, which was something that caught the attention of the writers, some of whom weren't very happy about it. But the A's had won the World Series in '72, and most of their players wore moustaches, so why couldn't we?

On the morning of March 5, we took a car from Schrafft's to Little Yankee Stadium, and we immediately noticed that there was a whole mob of reporters there, way more than usual. We couldn't even find a place to park in our lot right by the ballpark, because all the networks had vans there taking up space. When we finally parked and walked over to the ballpark, we couldn't even get inside for all the people there. A clubhouse attendant came out and said we couldn't come in. "Why?" we asked him. He told us that a major event had happened, and that Michael Burke and the whole Yankees front office was in there talking to the press. "Didn't you hear what happened?" he asked.

"No, what happened?"

"Mike Kekich and Fritz Peterson switched families." Thurman and I just looked at each other. We were stunned.

Fritz and Mike were two of the biggest pranksters on the team, and Thurman had been both a willing accomplice in their craziness and an unwilling victim, too. Thurman was self-conscious about his weight—"Squatty," "Tugboat," and even "Pudge" were among his less-flattering nicknames among our teammates—and Kekich would often slip Weight Watchers coupons into his locker. Thurman wore 38 waist uniform pants, but Kekich would always switch them out with 42 or 44 waist pants when he wasn't looking, just to mess with him. Fritz and Mike and Mel had also once teamed up to send Thurman a life-size sex doll, which showed up at the clubhouse in a giant box, already fully inflated. So our first thought when we heard about their wife-trade was that this was the craziest prank they'd pulled yet. It wasn't a prank, though. Mike and Fritz had switched wives, families, bank accounts, dogs, everything. We'd never seen anything like this in our whole lives. Left-handers are crazy, anyway, but this was like living in *The Twilight Zone*.

Kekich was a character and a half. Both him and Fritz were; Mark "The Bird" Fidrych was a normal human being compared to these two. I roomed with Kekich on the road sometimes, and it came back to me: The year before, when we were in Cleveland, I was sleeping and Mike came in, probably one o'clock in the morning. And all of a sudden, our phone rang, and Mike picked it up. I thought he was talking to Susan, his wife—but before he hung up, I heard him say, "I love you, Marilyn." It was the middle of the night and I'd been asleep, so I thought maybe I was imagining things. I wasn't, but I never put two and two together until that day in March '73, and that's when everything started to make sense.

We knew that Fritz and Mike had been great friends; they used to do everything together. But it was the furthest thing from our minds that something like *this* would happen. Looking back, though, you could see that it was all leading up to this. They did everything together, and were practically living in the same house together.

But now, nobody was talking about the coming season; everybody was talking about Peterson and Kekich, whether they're still friends or not friends. I guess they weren't talking to each other anymore, because even though Fritz took Mike's wife and Mike took Fritz's, it wasn't working out so well for Mike. To this day, Fritz is one of my best friends, and he's still with Susan. But the thing with Mike and Marilyn didn't last long.

Thurman and I never really talked about it between us, because everywhere we went for the rest of spring training and the '73 season, it seemed like someone wanted to ask us about it. People were gossiping about it in the clubhouse; whenever we were on the road, reporters from the local papers wanted to talk about "The Trade," the wife-swapping, more than the game or our team. And every time we'd go to the Stage Deli, people would ask us about it. We were sick of hearing about it, to be honest. We just wanted to play baseball!

A lot of people remember Fritz from the wife-swap, but they don't remember what a really good pitcher he was. He was one of the mainstays of our starting rotation; he won 20 games for the team in '70 and 17 in '72. Mike had a great arm, but Fritz really knew how to pitch. But Fritz struggled in '73, probably because of all the distractions, and ended up with an 8–15 record. Mike had an even worse season—in April, he got hit in the nuts with a line drive in batting practice, was out for over a month, and then pitched terribly when he came back. The Yankees got rid of him as soon as they could, trading him to the Indians in June.

We were so used to a hands-off organization, because CBS never bothered us, never touched us at all. Then all of a sudden, you've got this guy who was an athlete and a competitor, a guy who was a football coach (he was a graduate assistant to Woody Hayes at Ohio State and an assistant football coach at Northwestern and Purdue). George was the type of guy who would get in your face, and everybody was afraid of him. He buys the Yankees for $10 million with a group of people from Cleveland. He comes down and introduces himself to the team, and we're all thinking, "Wow, this guy is great! He's gonna do this for us and do this for us!" And then, two weeks later, he's in everybody's face.

When George came in as our new owner, it generated so much excitement—not just among the fans and the press, but among us players. Here comes a guy saying that he wanted the Yankees to be the Yankees again, to be a team New Yorkers could be proud of. He gave us a rah-rah pep talk when he bought the team. And from the very beginning, he gravitated toward Thurman. He knew Thurman was a leader, and that a lot of people gravitated toward him for leadership. I mean, if I had any questions about the team we were about to play, I would not go to Ralph Houk, I would go to Thurman. And it's not because we were best of friends; it was because he was our leader. Mentally, Thurman really was a level above other ballplayers. Instead of thinking two innings ahead, he could think five or six innings ahead, and George knew that about him from the beginning. Thurman was from Canton, George's ship-building company was in Cleveland, so they had that Ohio connection—but more than that, Thurman was happy because George was talking about building a winner.

We didn't know much about George when he came in, other than that he was in the shipping business. But he told us, "We're gonna make some great changes! Whatever this team needs, just let me take care of it."

And we thought, "Golly, this is great!" I actually thought George was Jewish, because of the "Stein" in Steinbrenner, so I was like, "A Jewish owner? This is wonderful!" Gabe Paul *was* Jewish, which a lot of people didn't know.

George didn't really show his toughness for the first few months he owned the team. The first time we really saw that side of him was after the Mayor's Trophy Game in May '73.

Every year, the Yankees would play the Mets in a game to raise money for charity, and that year they beat us 8–4 at Shea. We were a half game out of first in the AL East at the time, we'd just come off a tough road trip where we'd been swept by the White Sox, and the Orioles were coming to town to play us, so we could have used the day off. In fact, most of our regular starters didn't play that day, because Ralph wanted to give us a rest.

And that was when we saw George's real colors, because George let us know that he *never* wanted to lose to the Mets, even though it was just an exhibition game. It was a major thing with him. He wasn't at the game, but the next time we saw him in the clubhouse he was steaming. He told us, "You never, ever lose to that team!" That's when he really started showing us what a major hands-on guy he was, and that's when he and Ralph and Thurman and some of our other players started having disagreements with him. Unlike Michael Burke or Lee MacPhail, George would come down to the clubhouse all the time, and that's when he started stirring the pot. He was always saying things like, "If you don't want to play for me, get out!"

And he would tell us that he wanted each of us to always comport ourselves as a Yankee. He said, "I don't want to get calls at two in the morning telling me that I've gotta get you out of jail. If that happens, we're going to have problems."

George got into all our business. We always suspected that George had spies watching us. Whenever a guy we didn't know came into the clubhouse, like a mailman or a food delivery guy, we thought that he might spying for George. We never found out who the spies were, but we were pretty sure he had them, because he always seemed to know what we were doing and saying, even if weren't at the ballpark. He was more hands-on than hands-on.

Everyone was looking pretty hippie-ish at that time—even men who weren't hippies had long hair, and everybody was growing moustaches and beards. But George let it be known right away that he was totally against that, especially for players on our team. He wanted us to look "professional," and to him that meant no beards, no bushy sideburns, no hair below the collar line.

One day in June, I got to the clubhouse around 12:30 in the afternoon for a 7:30 night game. Thurman immediately came up to me in the clubhouse and said, "Did you get a letter from George?" I looked in my locker, and sure enough there was a letter from George, saying he needed to see me as soon as I got to the ballpark. Gene Michael (who we called "Stick") got one, too, and so had Graig Nettles. We'd gotten Nettles from Cleveland in the off-season, and he'd been a perfect addition to the team—"Puff," as we called him, had a powerful left-handed bat, and he was a dream to watch at third base.

We all wondered why we were getting called up to see George. I was having a great season, hitting .400 as the team's left-handed DH, Thurman was hitting around .300, and while Stick and Puff were struggling at the plate at the time, they still brought a lot to the team every day. So we know we're not getting released. But maybe we're getting traded?

So we go up together to see George, and his secretary, Doris, waves us into his office. We all go in, and he says, "Shut the door." Somebody shuts the door, and he says, "You know, the hair policy on our team is that you cannot have long hair, and you guys look really messy. I've got a barber that's coming by today, and you all have to get your hair cut."

Thurman was the first one to say anything. "George, there's no way I'm going to cut my hair," he said quietly, but you could tell he was pissed. I was more vocal about it—I told him, "Go eff yourself! I'm hitting .406. You gonna cut my hair, and I'm gonna be like Samson. You're not gonna do that! There's no way in the world I'm going to get a haircut!"

The other guys said pretty much the same things, and we all stomped out of there. What could George do, right? He's not going to get rid of an everyday catcher like Thurman; he's not gonna get rid of me, because I'm hitting the cover off the ball; and he's not gonna get rid of Stick and Puff, because that's the left side of our infield. But we were still a little nervous because we told him where to get off. At the very least, we figured, we were all gonna get fined.

We won the game that night, came back the next day, once again there's an envelope in our lockers from George. We open it, and there's $100 in there—everyone who'd been up there the day before got $100, which was a lot of money to us at a time when you had to really fight to get a $500 raise. There was also a note from George, which said, "I appreciate you coming up, and I appreciate you fighting for yourselves. I have more respect for you, because you fought for yourself and you fought for your teammates. Here's a hundred dollars to use as you wish."

And that was George in a nutshell. He was the kind of guy who wanted you to fight for yourself. If we'd gone in and said, "Okay, George, we'll get a haircut," he wouldn't have thought of us as leaders, or people who stood up for what they believed in. I normally wasn't the kind of guy to stir up any friction, but Thurman was, and George knew and respected that, even though they would fight a lot over the next five or six years.

George was tough, but he was good for the Yankees. He was honest about what he wanted from us—he wanted us to give 120 percent, and if you didn't do that, you were gone. We had fights and disagreements with him all the time; if you did something wrong, or something he didn't like, you'd hear about it. He wasn't a dictator, but he was a guy who refused to accept losing. And he and Thurman were on the same page that way; Thurman didn't care what your hair looked like, but he wanted you to care about winning the game, and he didn't want you to do anything stupid that might get in the way of that.

We had no idea how big the designated hitter thing was going to be when it was introduced in spring training, but it worked out pretty nicely for me in '73. I still played first base sometimes, but mostly I was in the lineup as the DH. I was hitting the ball really well that year, but even when my average was up around .406, Ralph wouldn't play me against left-handers. They sat me on the bench for that. All the writers were going nuts about it, and criticizing Ralph for it, but I never said anything, because I wasn't one of those guys who are going to cause problems. I just wanted to let my ability speak for me. But it was a done deal; in April, the Yankees had picked up Jim Ray Hart from the Giants, and he was our main DH against lefties from then on.

In addition to coming up to the plate four times a game, one of my duties as the DH was being the go-between for the guys on the team who really liked to bet on the horses. Thurman was one, Roy White was another. They would always have their racing forms out, looking at who was running that day at Monticello, Yonkers, and Aqueduct. They might say to me, "Yonkers—I want five dollars on so-and-so in the fifth race tonight." Once I got all their bets together, I would call from the clubhouse up to Doris, who, along with being Steinbrenner's secretary, also worked the switchboard during the ballgames, and she would patch me through to the racetracks so I could place the bets. And then the guys would check with me when they came in off the field to see how the horse did. I was the DH/horse guy. Sometimes they would win like $40 or $50, and that was big to them, though I never understood how they actually got paid because I wasn't a gambler myself. A lot of guys on the team liked to gamble, but we lived by the rule of no betting on baseball games. We never saw anybody doing that.

One of the nice things about being the DH is that, if you weren't feeling 100 percent, you could reserve your strength for when you went up to the plate, then come back and rest for a couple of innings. There was one time in '73 where we flew into Detroit for a four-game series—Friday, Saturday, and a double-dip on Sunday—and I had the flu real bad. I was sweating like a pig on the plane, and really, really hurting. Our trainer, Gene Monahan, took my temperature and it was 104. I really did not know if I was going to play the next day; I wanted to, of course, but I was so sick I couldn't even see straight.

We got to the Cadillac in Detroit, and I immediately went up to my room and went to sleep; Gene had given me some medication to let me sleep. But when I went out to the ballpark the next day, I was still really sick. Thurman had been watching me on the plane—while he was playing gin with Bobby Murcer, which was their big thing—so he knew I was feeling bad. He comes up to me while I'm lying on the training table with towels all around me, and he asks me, "How are you doing, Bloomie?"

"Oh, I'm dying, Thurman," I croak.

"Okay," he says, "let me tell you what I'm gonna do: I'm gonna give you something, and I want you to take it a half an hour before the game, and it's gonna make you feel good."

He gives me a small little pill. I have no idea what it is—I'm very naïve—so I just say, "Okay, yeah. Thanks, Thurman." Because the team is doing good, and I'm penciled into the lineup, and I've gotta play.

I guess it was maybe what they call a "greenie." Back then, basically 85–90 percent of the players took them. It was basically like a NoDoz. It wasn't like cocaine or steroids; it was just something to wake you up, like kids in college used to stay up studying for exams or like truckers used to keep away on the road. Everybody would talk in the clubhouse about how, "It's time to drink our cup of coffee." And when they'd do that, you knew what those guys were doing. If you took a greenie, then the coffee really would really boost it.

But I was naïve and had never done anything like that before. I took the pill that Thurman gave me, and all of a sudden I felt like I was in *The Jetsons!* It's like when Pete Rose used to run to first base on a walk faster than most people would try to beat out a base hit. I was wired like that! I felt great and ready to play. But when I got up to the plate, I was so hyper my hands were shaking, and the ball looked like three balls coming at me. I kept swinging and missing each time I came up. I don't know who was pitching, but I knew I looked like a fool swinging. I said, "Thurman, what did you *do* to me?"

He just laughed and said, "Now I know not to give one of those to you again. You were missing the ball by two or three feet!"

That night, I couldn't sleep; the next day, I was in the lineup again, and I struck out twice. I couldn't sleep for four days in a row! "What did you give me?" I kept asking him.

"I gave you some Indian medication," he replied. That's all he would say. From then on, I never took anything again. But Thurman would always tease me about it; we'd be hanging out talking to people at a bar or something, and he'd tell them, "Have Bloomie tell you about the time he couldn't sleep for four nights in a row!"

People nowadays say, "Oh, you guys took amphetamines," and make a big deal out of it, but a greenie really was like a NoDoz, something you could get over the counter. Drinking was much more of a thing in the days when we played, and all those guys who would drink after games, they'd need something to get them going the next day, especially when the day-to-day grind of the long season was wearing on them. You'd hear players saying, "I'm tired—I need to take a pepper-upper." But it wasn't like we had big jars of the stuff sitting out in the clubhouse.

I never saw Thurman take much of that stuff at all. Thurman would drink, like other ballplayers, but I never saw him do any drugs whatsoever. And as crazy as some of these guys were, I never saw any of them come into the clubhouse drunk. Even on road trips, I saw plenty of people hungover, but I never saw anyone take a drink during the game. But the NoDoz type stuff was common. A starting pitcher might take one a half hour before the game, or if a relief pitcher knows he might come in in the seventh, he'd take one in the fourth. That was a known fact. But even in my day, I never saw any player smoking grass or doing cocaine or any of that stuff. I would hear players talk about going to parties where that was going on. But I didn't hang around with people who did that stuff, and I never saw any ballplayers taking that stuff. But taking a pep pill, that was everyday life for lots of players.

But even with the number of games Thurman caught every season, he was more of a "natural high" guy. He was just always pumped up for a game, and I really don't think he had to take anything, because he was such an intense competitor; that was what he lived to do. And he was three lockers away, and we did pretty much everything together, so I'm sure I would've seen it if he was taking something like that on a regular basis.

Thurman liked to have a few beers after the game, or on a team flight, or if we'd go out at night, but I never saw him get really sauced. Sam McDowell, on the other hand, was known to be a major, major drinker. We got him in June '73 from the Giants, which was exciting for us because we had never had a real power pitcher on the staff, at least during the time I'd been with the team. Sam was a *big* guy, maybe 6'5", way over 200 pounds, and he'd led the league in strikeouts five times. When Sam was going good, he was incredible; he had a great arm and could throw a fastball over 100 miles an hour. That's why they called him "Sudden Sam." To this day, I'd swear he threw a little bit harder than Nolan Ryan, and Nolan threw like 100 to 103. And if he pitched a nine-inning game, he'd throw like

170 pitches, and still come back four or five days later ready for more.

But things weren't going so good for Sam by the time we got him. He joined our team while we were playing in Oakland, but he stayed in the hotel drinking for three days instead of coming to the ballpark. I went up to his hotel room to say hello, and it was just totally wiped out, filled with empty bottles, beer cans, the whole thing. He finally made it out to the airport for our flight to Anaheim, and he got on the airplane wearing an orange suit, holding a suitcase that said "Sudden Sam" on it. He looked like a giant orange.

About a month later, we're playing in Boston, and Thurman and I are walking back from Daisy Buchanan's about one thirty or two in the morning. All of a sudden, I see a guy lying in the gutter on Boylston Street wearing an orange suit, and you can really see it because it's fluorescent— it's an *orange* suit. Sure enough, it's Sam, and he's out cold, and it's starting to rain.

"We can't leave him here, Bloomie," Thurman mutters. We're tired and want to go to bed, and the last thing we want to do right now is pick up this huge guy and drag him several blocks back to the Sheraton Prudential, where we're staying. But he's our teammate, and a rainy gutter on Boylston is no place anyone should be at any hour of the day. We try to shake Sam awake, but no dice. We look for a cab, but there aren't any. "Help me lift him," Thurman says, trying to leverage Sam's huge frame into an upright position as the rain really starts coming down. We get him stood up, drape his arms over each of our shoulders, and start the slow trudge back to our hotel.

We get him back to the hotel, and we're all completely soaking wet now, because we had to walk four or five blocks carrying a gigantic guy who's been already lying in the gutter for a while. There's nobody even in the lobby at this point, so we prop Sam—who's still completely out of it—against the reception desk and ring the bell. Once the receptionist shows up, we find out that Sam hasn't even checked in yet; we'd checked in to the hotel when we'd gotten to town earlier that day, made sure our luggage was going up to our rooms, and then went straight to the ballpark. But Sam wasn't checked in, and we had no idea where his luggage was. Finally, we got him checked in, took him up to his room, and threw him in bed, and we got the bellman to find his bags and put them in his room. And then we went back to our own rooms to dry off and try and get some sleep.

The next day, Sam comes to the ballpark like it's no big deal—except he's got two black eyes, and he has no idea how that happened to him, and no memory at all of how he got back to the hotel, so he must have been waffled pretty good! We hadn't even noticed his black eyes the night before, because his hair was in his face and we were too focused on trying to get him back to the hotel. If he had stayed there all night in the gutter, who knows what could have happened to him?

Sam didn't pitch in that series against Boston, though he warmed up a few times. And then, as we're getting on the plane to Detroit, I look over and see that someone's crossed out the "Sudden" on his suitcase, and written "Seldom." It was funny, but it was also sad, because Sam could have been a Hall of Fame pitcher. He had the Hall of Fame arm, but not the head. Thurman used to yell at him all the time when he pitched for us, because Sam wanted to throw what he wanted to throw. Thurman would come back to the dugout and tell Ralph, "You better get him outta there. He's mixing me up because he's not looking at my signs—he just wants to throw!"

Ralph would tell Sam, "You need to look at Thurman's signs and throw the pitch he wants." But then he'd go back out there, and after a few pitches you'd see Thurman walking out to the mound pointing at him, like, "You listen to me! You don't listen to me, I'm gonna get you outta here!"

Thurman didn't have that problem with a lot of pitchers, but some pitchers just wanted to throw what they wanted to throw. They'd shake him off, but Thurman would never take that. He would go out there and tell them what to do. A lot of guys became pretty good pitchers from listening to Thurman. And the guys who didn't want to listen to Thurman, well, they got them outta there.

The Yankees eventually released Sam at the end of the '74 season, but he didn't do much good for us during the year and a half he was with the team, both because he wouldn't listen to Thurman, and because he was battling some serious demons. But I'm happy to say that he's turned his life around since then; he's a big guy with AA, and he's helped a lot of people.

We found Sam in the gutter on that same trip to Boston where Thurman had his infamous fistfight with Carlton Fisk. You can't talk about Thurman without talking about Fisk, though I'm sure if Thurman was still here he'd prefer that I didn't mention him. Even though he had a reputation for being gruff and mean, Thurman never feuded with anybody on or off the field, with one exception: Fisk.

It had all started in '72, when Fisk came up with the Red Sox as their hotshot new catcher and wound up winning Rookie of the Year *and* a Gold Glove, which Thurman had never won even though he was the better defensive catcher. The question was always being asked in the papers: Who was the best catcher, Munson or Fisk? We'd always tease Thurman by showing him articles from the paper that talked about how great Fisk was, and how much better he was than Thurman. Or when we were on the bus, we would always talk among ourselves about how Fisk was the best catcher in the American League, just loud enough for Thurman to hear us. And Thurman, oh god, it killed him; I mean, he would just say every swear word in the whole world, and throw things around like he was ready to destroy the whole bus. We would get on him like that, in a joking way, but it wasn't a joke to him. The first thing he'd do every day when he flipped to the box scores was to see how Fisk did the night before; and if Fisk had done well and Thurman had gone 0-for-4, he would fume and not say anything to anybody for hours.

Thurman absolutely hated Fisk. He *hated* him. They were totally different animals. Because Thurman was a blue-collar criminal behind the plate, a guy whose uniform was always out of place and looked like he hadn't shaved for a week, and Fisk was a guy whose uniform was perfect, never wanted to get dirty, had his hair perfect, and he always strode to the plate with a strut. And whenever he would step into the box while Thurman was catching, Thurman would grab a handful of dirt and throw it on his shoes and socks, just to get him dirty and mess him up.

Thurman never chewed tobacco, so he wouldn't spit tobacco juice into the batter's box like some catchers did back then. But with any guy he wanted to get on a little bit, he would pick up some dirt and throw it at his shoe, or kick dirt at them, because he knew a lot of batters don't like that. Thurman would also usually try to distract batters by talking to them, but I don't think he ever said anything to Fisk when he was up at the plate. He hated him so much, it was like he didn't even want to waste any words on him. But whenever we played the Red Sox, he would tell me, "Watch this fucking guy go down. I'm gonna make sure he doesn't have any hits. And if he comes close to me, I'm gonna ram his head and tear him up."

He finally got his chance to take on Fisk on August 1, 1973. Thurman was on third, and Stick tried to lay down a bunt on a suicide squeeze; Stick totally missed the pitch, but Thurman kept on heading home, and completely clocked Fisk when he got there. After the collision, Fisk came up swinging, Stick jumped on Fisk and everybody ran out on the field to mix it up. Even Ralph Houk got into the action! When they finally pulled Thurman out of the pile, I thought he was going to have an aneurysm; the veins were popping out of his neck, and flames were shooting out of his eyes. Before the game the next day, I saw Thurman watching Fisk take batting practice. "That schmuck," I heard him say to no one in particular. "If there's another fight today, I got him again!"

I think that if Thurman had lived, he would still hate Fisk today—and if Fisk died tomorrow, him and Thurman would have a fight up in heaven. There was just that much bad blood between them. They were both super catchers, obviously, but I would take Thurman over any catcher that I have ever seen, Fisk included. Not just because of his baseball ability—he was much better than Fisk at nailing base-stealers—but because of the way he worked with pitchers (Luis Tiant, who pitched for the Yankees in '79, has often told me that Thurman would be his number one choice to have behind the plate) and because of his leadership. He was totally the type of guy you'd go into the trenches for.

We hated all those guys on the Red Sox—Fisk, Yaz, Bill Lee, Rico Petrocelli, Rick Miller, Dwight Evans—but we loved playing them. Whether they were playing us at Yankee Stadium or we were playing them at Fenway, it was always an event, and those games were the best. We *lived* for those games! Whenever we got our schedule for the season, the first thing we'd do is find out when the Red Sox games were. It was the best rivalry in the game! They hated us, too; even their writers hated us, and our writers hated their writers, and both of them were always trying to get quotes from us that would stir up the rivalry further.

But even though we had some good fights with them, the best fights in the world were the ones in the stands during Red Sox–Yankees games. You wouldn't believe all the fights! We used to watch the action from the dugout. I'll never forget, we were playing the Red Sox at Yankee Stadium one time, and all of a sudden, we see all these police running to the seats behind home plate where the wives usually sat. Our wives had been saying stuff to their wives, and it got out of hand—it was like the Civil War, the North against the South, our wives against their wives!

There were always wild fights in the upper deck at Yankee Stadium between Yankee and Red Sox fans. Ralph would look up at them and say, "Those guys are gonna fall onto the field!" Oh, how they wailed on each other! You'd see hot dogs, hamburgers, peanuts, and popcorn flying up in the air, people dumping sodas and beers on each other, and the ushers running to the section. It was incredible.

I think most of the guys on the team loved to play in Boston, even though the dugout and clubhouse were terrible. I know Thurman did. It was such a great ballpark to play in, with the Green Monster and with the stands so close to the field. And so many Yankees fans would make the trip from

New York to see us play. Of course, their fans hated us. It was mostly college kids out in the center-field bleachers at the time, and they would always yell things at us and throw stuff at us— cups, papers, hot dog wrappers. And in right field, the first six or seven rows would always be filled with the betting guys; they would bet on everything that was happening during the game, even what we did in BP. I'd be out there in right shagging balls, and I could see and hear everything they were doing because they were so close to the field.

At Fenway, you could hear everything the fans yelled at you; the on-deck circle was like five feet from the stands. But I liked it when they got on me, because that meant they knew I was a good player. And when Thurman got up, oh they would just rain abuse on him. Even when he was taking batting practice, it would be, "BOOOOOO!!!"

The visitors' dugout was so tiny and cramped, and the clubhouse always stunk because it was so small— it was like having 25 sweaty guys crammed into your living room. But when you went out onto the field, it was as thrilling as being in Yankee Stadium. You could feel all the history there; you could see the Jimmy Fund sign and the seat where Ted Williams' longest home run landed. One time, Thurman, myself, and a couple of other guys went back inside the scoreboard in the Green Monster, and they showed us how they put up the runs and hits by hand. They showed us how they worked the whole thing, and it was so fascinating, like going back in time!

Whenever we'd play in Boston, we'd usually go to Daisy Buchanan's after the games to drink some beers—and when the Yankees were in town, there would be extra police there, just in case anybody tried to start trouble. And we'd usually wind up having some words with some Red Sox fans there, but it was fun. Sometimes we'd run into Red Sox players at the Boston bars, but we wouldn't talk to each other; whenever we played in Oakland, we'd usually end up having drinks with some of the A's guys like Gene Tenace, Joe Rudi and Sal Bando, but we didn't have that kind of relationship with the Boston guys, except Luis Tiant. You couldn't hate Luis, because you could never find a better human being than him; he was the type of guy who would talk to anybody. We could never seem to beat Luis in Boston, but the one time we did—and I should add, we won in 12 and Luis didn't even take the loss—Thurman and I walked into a bar afterward and saw him sitting there by himself. I called out, "Hey, Luis!" and we sat down at the table with him. Without saying a word, he got up, went to another table, and spent the rest of the night sitting with his back to us.

A lot of the guys used to walk to Fenway from the Sheraton Prudential—it was only about a mile—and walk back afterward. We usually wouldn't hang around the hotel, because there were so many fans there, and they'd want to sit down next to you at lunch or in the lobby and ask to hear all these stories. So we'd walk around town, and people knew who we were; even the shopkeepers would talk smack to us.

Thurman loved it, though. It was such a baseball town, and he loved how much passion the fans had for the game.

The Yankees and the Red Sox is one of the greatest rivalries in sports, and it's a monster that Thurman and Fisk really helped create. In '75 and '76, Thurman actually caught both ends of a few of our doubleheaders with them. Even though they were in the middle of summer, he had to play those games, both because he wanted to be in on the action as much as possible—and because he knew Fisk would never catch both ends.

Aside from the Red Sox, I always liked talking to players on other teams, whether it was at a bar, standing on first base during the game, or while running in the outfield during pregame warmups. Nolan Ryan was always one of the friendlier opposing players I encountered, but boy was he tough on us. The first time I faced him, in '72, I hit a homer off him—it landed in the third deck in right field—but I didn't get another extra-base hit off him for six years. Thurman never got so much as a single extra-base hit off him, and Thurman was the type that almost always got the bat on the ball. Nobody liked to face Nolan.

Nolan threw hard and he threw fast, and people would sometimes ask me if it made me nervous to step in against him. I was never nervous against him or any other pitcher—

I'm up there to hit, and I want them to be nervous of me, nervous of what I can do if I get ahold of a pitch. Thurman was the same way; he was up there to hit. The worst you could do to us is make us look bad on a third strike, or get us to hit into a double play. But with one swing of the bat, we could put a run on the board, or more if anyone was on base at the time. You could get us out, but we could *beat* you. That was the attitude we always took up to the plate. Our goal was to be as focused as possible; you've got the ball coming in at 95–100 miles an hour, and you have to concentrate. And against Nolan, you *really* had to concentrate.

Nolan was chasing Koufax's strikeout record in '73, and he almost no-hit us on August 29. In the first inning, with one out and Roy White on first, Thurman hit a pop fly out past second that Rudy Meoli and Sandy Alomar got crossed up on, and it dropped for a hit. And that was it for us; we struck out 10 times—he rang up Thurman and I once apiece—and we didn't get a hit the rest of the way. If one of those guys had caught Thurman's pop fly, it would have been Nolan's third no-hitter of the season!

Back then, if we were facing a great pitcher like Nolan Ryan—or Luis Tiant or Jim Palmer or Dave McNally—we knew that the umpire was going to give them a break. They'd proven themselves to be among the best of the best, so they'd get a little more leeway on the corners, or whatever. And the umpires were the same way with Thurman, because they knew he knew how to call the game. And they knew that Thurman would very rarely show them up over balls and strikes, whereas some catchers like Fisk would pull their masks off and turn around and start yelling at them. But Thurman never embarrassed an umpire like that, and umpires respected that. If an umpire missed the pitch, Thurman might say something under his breath like, "You missed that one," and the umpire would say, "I'll make it up to you."

If we had some free time on the road, like if a game got rained out or we'd played a day game and there was nothing to do at night in that city, Thurman and I would sometimes go to the movies together. For us, the best movie of '73 was *Bang the Drum Slowly*—not just because it was a great baseball story, but because we were also in it!

We knew they'd filmed much of the movie at Yankee Stadium and at Shea Stadium in '72, but we had no idea they were going to use footage from our games, as well. Robert DeNiro played the catcher in the film, and he wore Thurman's number 15 behind the plate, and the team's first baseman had number 12 like I did. We thought that was a great coincidence, but then we actually saw ourselves on the screen! Thurman was in two of the shots—he was shown throwing somebody out at second base, and then there was a shot of a runner sliding into him as he blocked the plate. And then there was a short clip of me, making a pretty good running catch over my shoulder in right field. It was a really sad movie, but we walked out with smiles on our faces. "Y'know, Bloomie," Thurman laughed as we were leaving the theater, "We sure looked pretty good up there!"

We'd also kill time on the road going to record stores. We all had little tape players or boomboxes, and we would always buy cassettes because they were easier to carry around and listen to on the road. Nat Tarnopol always made sure we had the latest cassettes from Brunswick, and Michael Grossbardt, who did all the photos for the Yankees programs and yearbooks, was the son of the guy who owned Colony Records, a big music store at the corner of Broadway and 49th in Manhattan. We used to go down to Colony and load up on tapes; it was great.

One tape Thurman and I listened to a lot that summer was *The Captain and Me* by The Doobie Brothers, who were one of Thurman's favorites. "Long Train Running" and "China Grove" were the big hits off that album, but we also listened a lot to the song "The Captain and Me." The song was long, and the words were pretty cosmic; it was definitely a whole other kind of thing than the songs by The Intruders or The Stylistics or The Chi-Lites that I loved to listen to, but I liked the positive message they seemed to be putting across. It was a song about people coming together to change things for the better; Thurman was not yet officially our team captain, but we all thought of him as our leader, and the song made me think of that day when we'd finally get our World Series ring, the Captain and me.

Ron finished the 1973 season with a .329 average, which would have been good enough for second place in the American League behind the .350-hitting Rod Carew, if only he'd had enough plate appearances to qualify. As it was, his 12 home runs and career-high 57 RBIs were solid indeed for a player who'd only appeared in 100 games and walked to the plate 338 times. Thurman got his own average back up to .301 in 1973, while reaching what would be career highs in doubles (29) and home runs (20), scoring 80 times, knocking in 74 runs, and winning what would be the first of three consecutive Gold Gloves as a catcher. (His archrival Carlton Fisk would never win another.)

From late April to the middle of August, the Yankees were rarely more than a game or two out of first place, and they even spent 52 days atop the American League East. But despite having a talented team—one clearly improved by the additions of Graig Nettles and talented young starting pitcher George "Doc" Medich—the Yankees stumbled badly from mid-August onward, winding up with an 80–82 record and a fourth-place finish, 17 games behind the pennant-winning Baltimore Orioles. Meanwhile, across town, the 82–79 Mets finished first in the National League East, beat the favored Cincinnati Reds in the

NL playoffs, and took the defending World Champion Oakland A's to seven games in the World Series before giving up the ghost.

George Steinbrenner, who could not stand the idea of the Mets receiving more attention than his Yankees, surely would have spent the winter chewing out Ralph Houk, if the Major— who loathed Steinbrenner almost as much as Steinbrenner loathed the Mets—hadn't pre-empted such unwelcome phone calls by quitting at the end of the season. Though Nat Tarnopol was still smarting over being rejected as a suitor for the Yankees, he tried to help his pal Dick Williams (who had already planned to leave the A's and their bellicose owner Charlie O. Finley at the end of the postseason) snag the vacant Yankees managerial spot. Following the World Series, Williams announced to the press that he would be wearing Yankee pinstripes in 1974, but Finley had other ideas.

We were all really sad to see Ralph go. To us, Ralph *was* the Yankees. He had begun managing the team in '61, then he'd been in the front office for a few years in the mid-60s, and then he came back as the manager in '66 and had been there ever since. He'd been the only major league manager that Thurman and I had ever known, and we both learned so much from him. He'd been a catcher as well, and he and Thurman used to sit and talk about catching for hours. They were both hard-nosed, blue-collar guys, and they had a lot of respect for each other.

But Ralph had to leave, because he finally couldn't take George anymore. George was always calling him up, telling him how to run the ballclub, calling him at home, calling him in the dugout. He would always be telling Ralph, "You've gotta do this" or "You've gotta do that." It got to the point where George was trying to set the pitching rotation for us. "You need to let *this* guy pitch!" For all our frustration with CBS, at least they'd let Ralph run the show. But with George, that was simply not an option.

We still hung out with Nat all the time, even though we'd been warned by the Yankees to stay away from him. And even though George had managed to buy the team that Nat wanted to buy, Nat remained a Yankee fan and wanted to see us win, which was why he put George in touch with Dick Williams. George loved the idea of having Williams manage us, because he had a fiery personality and a proven track record of winning. We knew Williams a little bit through Nat, and were looking forward to playing for him. Unfortunately, Charlie Finley said Williams still had a year left on his A's contract, and told the Yankees he wasn't going to let Williams out of it unless they traded the A's two of our hot prospects, Scotty McGregor and Otto Velez, in return. And Gabe Paul wasn't going to allow that, so the search was on for a new skipper.

What would '74 bring? We knew we were going to be playing our home games at Shea Stadium, and we knew we were going to be playing for a manager who wasn't Ralph Houk or Dick Williams. And I can't say Thurman or I were very happy about either of those things.

7

Trade Me to Cleveland

After months of unsuccessfully trying to pry Dick Williams from Charlie Finley's grasp, the Yankees resolved their managerial shortage on January 3, 1974, signing Bill Virdon to a one-year contract as the team's skipper. Virdon, who had led the Pittsburgh Pirates to an NL East title in 1972, had been fired by the Bucs in September 1973 after a disappointing and tumultuous season, during which he'd clashed with several of the team's players. Despite this, and despite the fact that many saw Virdon's hiring as an interim stopgap until the Williams situation could be resolved in the Yankees' favor, George Steinbrenner spoke highly of his new manager. "He's a winner, and that's the kind of man we wanted," he told the press when Virdon's hiring was announced.

But after being managed for so many seasons by the calm and fatherly Ralph Houk, many Yankees players would have difficulty adjusting to Virdon's more rigid and impersonal style.

Many would find it even more difficult to adjust to their Shea Stadium exile. But despite these obstacles—and some serious roster shakeups courtesy of Steinbrenner and Gabe Paul— the 1974 Yankees would distinguish themselves as one of the toughest teams in the American League.

Thurman didn't like Virdon that much, and never really got along with him. A lot of guys didn't, because most of us had come up with Ralph, and everybody loved him. Ralph was a tough manager, but he was fair; Virdon was just strict, and he worked us much harder during spring training than Ralph ever did. Which was funny, because Ralph was "the Major," who had been an Army officer during World War II, but Virdon had much more of a "military" approach to things than Ralph did.

Virdon had been a really good outfielder with the Pirates, and he'd had some success with them as a manager, but there was no connection with the Yankees, whereas we all thought of Ralph as a true Yankee. Virdon was just a guy they hired because they couldn't get Dick Williams. I think Williams would have been a better fit for the team, personality-wise, but Finley wouldn't let him go, so we got Virdon. And Virdon brought in Mel Wright, his right-hand man, to be our new bullpen coach, and most of our pitchers did not get along with Mel Wright. So it was a major transition for us.

Me, I got along okay with Virdon, and thought he generally treated me pretty fairly. We called him "Popeye" behind his back, because he had these gigantic forearms. Ralph always had complete confidence in Thurman's ability to call a game and handle the pitchers, but now Thurman was working with a manager who wasn't always on the same page as him, and he was pretty unhappy about that.

The team had a much different feeling with Virdon there, but it wasn't entirely his fault. We were playing at Shea Stadium, and that wasn't the greatest thing in the world. The ballpark was built on a landfill, on a marsh, and when it rained there it really stunk, especially in the dugout and the clubhouse. We had to use the New York Jets' clubhouse, and it always smelled like mildew down there. It was really cramped, too. When the Yankees picked up Alex Johnson later in the season, his locker was right next to me; Alex was a big guy, and we couldn't hardly get dressed at the same time.

Oh, Shea Stadium was the pits! Yankee Stadium was pretty run down when I started playing there, but it was still a beautiful stadium, and it felt magical. Shea had no magic at all. Shea was a dump. Their PA system was terrible, and you couldn't hear it most of the time anyway because you had airplanes going over the stadium every 30 seconds, flying to and from LaGuardia Airport, at what looked like only a few hundred feet above you. They were flying so low, it looked like you could reach up and touch the planes!

Our pitchers hated to pitch there because of all the noise from the planes, and it was tough to see there as a hitter, because there wasn't much of a background in center. The stadium was completely open behind the outfield fences, so it would get really windy there. Yankee Stadium, even though it was open, had the tall façade and the outfield bleachers, which made it feel less open and helped cut down on the wind.

The field was really poorly maintained, too. That's where Elliott Maddox had his accident in center field. He was a super ballplayer, a great athlete, but the outfield had sprinkler heads sticking out all over the place, and he tripped over one in '75 and hurt his knee, and it destroyed his career. He wound up suing the Mets over that (along with the Yankees, the American League, and the City of New York); I think the case went on for like 10 years, and he finally lost.

Playing at Shea really hurt Bobby Murcer's career, too. He might have been a Yankee for life if he hadn't had such a huge power drop off in '74. He hit in the third and fourth spots in our lineup, but he hit only two home runs at Shea all year. Yankee Stadium had that short porch in right, but right field was deeper at Shea, and you always had wind blowing in which didn't make it a good fit for power hitters like Bobby.

The plane noises were a constant distraction for hitters, too. We always wound up stepping out of the box and waiting for the plane to pass overhead, because those loud jet noises would mess with your concentration. If you're up there trying to drive a runner in, and here comes a plane that sounds like it's breaking the sound barrier, it can really take your mind off what you're trying to accomplish.

Obviously, Thurman had the hand signals to communicate with the pitcher, but the noise from the planes made it harder for him to concentrate on calling the game. And Thurman had a rough time of it in '74 anyway, because he'd hurt his hand in a spring exhibition game. He played through the pain, of course, but the injury nagged him all season, and negatively affected his hitting and his throwing. He still played in 144 games that year, though. You just could not get him out of the lineup for very long.

We definitely felt like stepchildren to the Mets when we were playing at Shea, and a lot of our fans didn't want to make the trip from the Bronx to Flushing Meadows to see us play. I'm told that we actually drew about the same amount of fans at Shea in '74 as we did at Yankee Stadium the year before, but it sure didn't feel like it. The place always seemed really quiet and empty when we were playing there. It was like playing out in the pasture somewhere. At least we had a place to play, but it was far from ideal. We knew it was just going to be two years and then it was going to be over with; it was just a matter of getting through it. What else could you do?

There were some positive developments for us that spring, though, like Lou Piniella joining us. The Yankees had picked him up in the off-season, and he fit right in with us. He was a funny guy, a really good hitter, and he and Thurman bonded because they had the same kind of intensity; they were both the type of guys who loved to get their uniforms dirty. And like with Thurman, you had to be real careful about what you said to Lou after he'd had a bad game, because you never knew how he was going to react. Thurman usually kept it inside, but Lou could go nuts real bad, like to the point where you were worried he might break a bat over somebody's head.

I'll never forget, one time we lost a ballgame in Cleveland, and both Lou and Thurman had a bad day. Playing at Cleveland Municipal Stadium was always pretty depressing. It was this huge, ugly, prehistoric stadium—they called it "the Mistake by the Lake"—that could fit like 80,000 people. But nobody was ever there in the stands, so it always felt very doom and gloom. There was always this one guy out in the bleachers banging away on his tom-tom, and you could hear it echoing all over the park. If you had a bad game there, the depressing atmosphere just made it seem worse. Losing a game in Cleveland, and then having to go back into the clubhouse and eat those lousy ham and cheese sandwiches they'd put out, it was pretty much the worst thing in the world.

In Cleveland, when you go from the clubhouse to the field, you've gotta go through this long, dark tunnel with all these bare lightbulbs on each side. Well, after this ballgame was over, Lou and Thurman were walking up the tunnel after the game with their bats, both of them in a really bad mood, and all of a sudden they started smashing the lightbulbs; it must have been 25 lights on each side of the tunnel, and they broke every single one. The next day, Virdon sat us down and gave us a stern lecture before the game: "Do not break the lights in the runway!"

Thurman and Piniella had lockers right next to each other, and their corner of the locker room was like a pigsty; they were like the dirtiest guys you'd ever seen. Piniella, if we had like a two-week road trip, he'd bring all his dirty clothes with him and just pile them up in his locker with his suitcase. Thurman was basically the same way. He would have all this crumpled clothing in there with his gloves and balls. It was a mess.

At the end of April, the Yankees did a trade with Cleveland that caught everybody by surprise: They sent Fritz Peterson, Steve Kline, Fred Beene, and Tom Buskey to the Tribe for Chris Chambliss, Dick Tidrow, and Cecil Upshaw. The Yankees had made a lot of deals in '73, but they were mostly pretty small. This Cleveland trade was the first time where we really saw what kind of lengths George and Gabe Paul were willing to go to in order to turn us into a contender—except a lot of us didn't see it that way at the time, because it felt like they were breaking up our family. Everybody was shouting at Gabe and Virdon in the clubhouse when we found out; Mel Stottlemyre and Bobby Murcer were really angry, and so was Thurman. To him, the Yankees had just given up the core of our staff by trading Fritz, Freddy, and Steve away.

Fritz had been one of our best, most reliable pitchers for years, but he'd had a bad '73 and the Yankees wanted to get rid of him because of all the "wife-swap" distractions. Freddy Beene was a good relief pitcher, and everybody really loved him because Freddy was a guy that could pitch in any type of a game, in any situation; I saw him come in once in the second inning and hang on to finish the game. He was a little guy, but he was tough. He was like a right-handed Sparky Lyle, but as a middle reliever who also did spot starts. And Steve Kline was a good pitcher who was very, very good friends with all the guys because he'd come up in the Yankee organization. He was especially close to Mel and Bobby and Thurman, who told the writers, "I'll go to Cleveland, too—they can trade me there now!" He was that angry.

I was upset too, and not just because Fritz and those guys were gone. I used to hit Dick Tidrow better than any other pitcher I faced; he was one of those guys I always looked forward to stepping in against, because when "Dirt" was with Cleveland I rapped him pretty good, and now I couldn't hit off him anymore. He wound up doing well for us in New York, though, and so did Chris, who had some real good years as a Yankee. I think Gabe knew we had a pretty good team, but we still had a ways to go to becoming a World Series–level team, and he knew that those guys would be important building blocks to a championship. It's tough to go through changes in your family like that, but it ended up being a good trade. A month later, another familiar face left us, when the Yankees sold Horace Clarke to the Padres. It was sad to see Hoss go, but we had to trust that George and Gabe had a plan.

When the big deal with Cleveland happened, that was the first time Thurman had ever made a "trade me to Cleveland"-type comment, and it wouldn't be the last. Thurman was from Canton, Canton was close to Cleveland, and Thurman's major thing was being a homebody guy. I mean, he *loved* Canton. Diana, their kids, and all of Diana's family were there, and Diana couldn't be in New York with him all the time. So, from then on, whenever Thurman was unhappy about the way things were going on the Yankees, or felt George or Gabe were disrespecting him, Thurman would tell the writers, "I want to go to Cleveland." It was always on his mind as an option. It wasn't about wanting to play on a different contender, because you'd never hear him say, "Send me to Baltimore," or "Send me to Oakland"—which would have made more sense, because those were the two best teams in the American League at the time. It was just an out for him. If something was going wrong, if he got his feelings hurt, it was always "Trade me to Cleveland." But I don't believe that Thurman ever really wanted to leave New York. And the Yankees would have never traded him.

Thurman was one of the few guys on the team who actually liked going to Cleveland for a series, because it meant he could go see his family and friends. For the rest of us, there really wasn't much to do there, so we were always happy when it was time to get out of town. Chicago, though, was always a favorite destination. We would stay at the Executive House down by the Chicago River, which was like a 20-minute bus ride from Comiskey Park, and only 10 minutes by cab from Rush Street, where all the bars were. We'd get back to the hotel after a night game, and by 11:00 we'd already be over on Rush or the nearby intersection of State and Division, looking at all the girls. Or we would go to the Pump Room at the Ambassador Hotel, which had great food and a great bar, and right across the street was Hugh Hefner's place, the Playboy Mansion, which was fenced in.

One night, me, Thurman, Stottlemyre, and somebody else, maybe Piniella, were leaving the Pump Room—it was probably about one in the morning—and we were walking back towards State and Division to look for a cab back to the hotel. We passed this little side street joint, and somebody said, "Hey, let's go in here and get one more drink."

We walked into this place, and it was really dark in there, even spooky a little bit. They had a guy playing piano, but other than that it was kind of quiet. It seemed like a nice place, though, so we grabbed a big booth in the corner, ordered a round of drinks, looked around, and realized it was all women in there, which seemed unusual. Two or three of them came over and sat down with us. They asked us to dance, but we weren't dancers, so we declined. Then they started flirting with us, trying to hold our hands and stuff and cuddle up next to us. They weren't bad looking, but we got a little bit uneasy when we realized they were all taller than we were. And then it clicked—we were in a transvestite bar! We paid the check and ran out of that place; we didn't even finish our drinks. "I just wanted another beer," Thurman laughed as we scrambled into the nearest cab.

Even though a lot of Yankee fans didn't like making the trip out to Shea, Nat Tarnopol would come out to all our games there. I also used to leave tickets for Jay Black, of Jay and the Americans, and Frankie Valli of The Four Seasons and Tommy James from The Shondells. Those guys came to just about every game we played at Shea. I was very close with them, and Thurman was, too.

Jay was a dear, dear friend of mine. I met Jay down at the Fontainebleau in Miami, when I went to see him perform during spring training one year. Somebody knew I was a big Jay Black fan, and told Jay that I was in the audience. And Jay started talking about me from the stage because he was a big fan of mine. He was Jewish, and his parents had wanted him to be a rabbi. So my wife and I went backstage, and we found out that he was from Howard Beach and still lived in New York. We started hanging out with him and his wife. And through Jay, I met Tommy James and Frankie Valli.

The three of them would sit together at the ballpark, and they all had these tiny vials of cocaine around their necks, and they would carry these small snub-nose revolvers in these little holsters that were wrapped around their socks, in case they had any "problems." So yeah, they were bringing cocaine and guns to the ballpark with them, and they would get high at the baseball game.

I actually never knew that they carried guns, until we were sitting at a restaurant one time, and Jay sat down next to me and I noticed a big bulge around his ankle. I said, "Jay, what is that?"

"Oh, that's my gun."

I said, "What?"

"Yeah," he said, "we always carry guns. Everybody in the record business does."

Jay had a Hall of Famer voice—he never even warmed up before he went out to sing. But Jay was involved with a lot of people who were "involved," so to speak; people like John Gotti and the Gambino family. Jay was a major gambler, and Frankie Valli and Tommy James, those guys were big gamblers at the time too, but not like Jay. Jay used to make like $10,000–$15,000 per appearance, and then he'd gamble it all away the next day. Gotti used to come to our games, too, because he was real good friends with Jay. He wasn't a major mobster back then, just a soldier in the Gambino family.

Thurman and I used to go have dinner at Jay's house in Howard Beach, and there would always be these very big Italian guys there making spaghetti and meatballs, and everybody would eat. Again, Thurman and I were kind of naïve about who these people were—we knew they were tough guys, but we didn't know what kind of stuff they were involved in. Thurman came from tough people in Canton, so he knew how to handle himself in this kind of crowd. Me, being from the South, this was all really new to me. These guys were all big Yankee fans, though, and they wanted to hang out with us and talk baseball. They never put the muscle on us, or anything. We were just novelties to them.

All those guys liked to talk baseball with us. I remember this guy named Anthony Ruggiano, who they called "Fat Andy"—I found out later that he was one of the major people with the Gambinos—got into this heated discussion with Marty Appel, who was the Yankees' PR guy, talking about who was better: Babe Ruth or Mickey Mantle. Fat Andy kept saying Babe Ruth was better, and Marty kept say, "No, Mickey Mantle!" They just kept going back and forth like that, and I thought Fat Andy was gonna get angry, but it thankfully never really escalated beyond that.

One night, Jay, myself, Marty Appel, and Fat Andy, we all got picked up at Jay's house by a big limousine, and it took us to a restaurant down in Little Italy. There was no place to park, but the limo pulled up right in front of the restaurant; we were blocking a major street, stopping all this traffic, but when the police came by to see what's going on, they just left us alone after they found out who we were.

It's an Italian restaurant, and it's really busy. I'm naïve, I think we're going to eat dinner. They show us into a smaller room in back, which is almost like another restaurant for mob-type guys, and Marty and I sit down at a table, while Jay and Fat Andy go into an office that was off of it. Before we can even get a menu, they come back out carrying a big suitcase; they hadn't come in with a suitcase, but they're leaving with one. "We gotta go now," they tell us. So we get back in the limo, and we get like a police escort out of there.

We get back to Jay's house, they open up the suitcase, and there's like thousands of dollars in the thing. It was like something out of a movie. It was just like an errand they were running, and they took us along with them. Marty said to me later, "You know, we could have gotten killed down there!"

We told Thurman about it the next day, and he just laughed. "That's one dinner I'm glad I missed," he said.

In '74, Thurman was voted the American League's starting catcher in the All-Star Game for first time, which was a huge honor for him (and he doubled and scored a run in the game). But he struggled a lot that season, and he was more unpleasant than usual with the writers as a result. If Thurman was walking around after the game with a beer in his hand, that was a good sign; but there were times where he'd just sit by his locker with his face turned toward the wall, lost in a foul mood, and god help you if you made the mistake of saying something to him when he was sitting like that. I saw him jump down more than a few writers' throats that season.

Around fans, though, Thurman was still wonderful. If we were out at the Stage Deli or another restaurant and somebody came up and asked him for an autograph, he would always oblige, unless of course he was in the middle of eating. Even five seasons into his major league career, he was still thrilled that fans wanted his autograph. We were some of the most popular players on the team, and people greeted us with smiles and open arms wherever we went in New York, and that always made us feel great, even when we were slumping on the field. And of course, when we were hanging out at Nat's office, and Nat would ask us to sign baseballs for his friends in the music industry, we were always happy to do it.

Thurman never liked to publicize it—in fact, I don't think he would even tell Diana when we were doing it—but he and I used to go around to hospitals in the city and visit the kids there. We'd go to places like Sloan-Kettering or Lenox Hill; we'd load ourselves up with a bunch of baseballs, then sign 'em and hand 'em out to the kids. You should have seen how great Thurman was with these kids, too; his whole attitude would change, because he loved to see kids laughing and playing, and he would do whatever he could to get them to smile. He'd joke around with them, and he'd say things like, "The next hit I get, that one's for you," or, "The next time I throw out a guy who's trying to steal, that's for you." And the kids loved him, because around them he would turn into a big, soft teddy bear. But most people never saw that side of him, and the writers probably wouldn't have even recognized the guy he was around those kids. I remember leaving one of the childrens' cancer wards with him, and he was just about in tears. I could tell he wanted to say something to me about how much it hurt him to see those poor, sick kids, but it wasn't his style to open up like that, even to a close friend like me. "That's tough," was all he could say. "That's tough."

Jerry Moses had been Thurman's backup in '73, but the Yankees sent him to Detroit in '74 as part of the trade that brought us Walt "No Neck" Williams, and Rick Dempsey took over the backup catcher position. Rick would catch the second game of a doubleheader or whenever Thurman needed a break. Rick had an unbelievable arm—he had a gun, one of the best arms I'd ever seen. He didn't have Thurman's quick release, but he was really accurate. He was a very good catcher, and Thurman taught him a lot about how to call a game. Thurman was an All-Star catcher, but he also knew that Dempsey would take his job in a second if he could; that's just how it was. But Thurman worked with him all the time, teaching him about blocking balls and working with pitchers, and he helped make Dempsey a very good catcher. Dempsey became a star after he was traded to the Orioles in '76, when he finally got the chance to catch every day.

Another great, underrated player who came to the team in '74 was Alex Johnson. He'd been the AL batting champ with the Angels in '70, and the Yankees had originally tried to get him back in '71 around the time I came up to the team, but they couldn't work out a deal. Late in the '74 season, though, they finally picked him up.

AJ had a bad reputation by the time he came to the Yankees. He'd had a weird incident in the Angels clubhouse where Chico Ruiz pointed a gun at him, and he'd clashed with several of the managers he'd played for. The Angels clearly did not know how to handle AJ, and it went real bad for him there. But let me tell you something—if and when he wanted to play, you couldn't find a better athlete.

Everybody talks about how tough he was, but AJ just wanted his peace. He was a very intelligent guy who just wanted people to leave him alone. He could just look at the writers and they'd run in the opposite direction! But his and No Neck Williams' lockers were right next to mine, and the three of us became great friends. We'd sit there in the mildewy clubhouse at Shea listening to my soul cassette tapes, just relaxing and talking. I asked him once, "AJ, what's your philosophy of hitting?"

He told me, "I hit when I want to. You hit what you can." That's how he saw it.

He was usually playing left field or DH with us, and I have never in my life seen anyone leave the ballpark quicker after a game; he was almost totally undressed before he got to the dugout! He'd go the locker room, take a shower before hardly anybody was in there, and he was driving out of the parking lot before the fans were even in their cars. But he could play, he could run, he could hit, he could do anything with the bat. He was so talented. Thurman used to marvel at him, and say to me, "What an incredible athlete!"

AJ was the greatest guy, very kind and funny once you got past the hard shell. I loved him, and Thurman loved him, but he was the one guy in the clubhouse that we never teased or made fun of, because he was like a piece of dynamite; if you lit that fuse, you didn't know when it was going to blow. But he was a really great teammate and a smart ballplayer, and Thurman had a lot of respect for him, even though the way he played could be frustrating to watch. Like, if AJ hit the ball back to the pitcher, he wouldn't even run to first base; he'd just take two steps, turn around, and head back to the dugout. But if he was close to a base hit, you couldn't get him; if he thought he had a chance to get a hit, he'd put on that speed and beat the throw to first.

There was one time where AJ hit a high pop to the outfield, and the left fielder and center fielder collided and the ball dropped, but since he'd taken his time getting down to first, he only had a single when he should have had a double. Thurman said something to him about it, but not in a way that would embarrass him in front of anybody—they passed each other going back onto the field, and I saw Thurman saying something short and to the point to AJ in a way that wouldn't draw anyone's attention to it. And AJ just nodded his head and didn't say anything. If you were someone that AJ didn't respect, or you showed him up in public, he'd fight you right then and there. But AJ always respected Thurman, and after Thurman called him out about something, he would never do it again.

Probably the craziest thing we saw all season was Graig Nettles and his superball bat. Puff had started the season really hot, hitting 11 homers in April, and people were talking about him breaking Roger Maris's record, but then he kind of tailed off before finding his power again in September—which, maybe coincidentally, was the time he started using his new bat.

We were playing a doubleheader against the Tigers at Shea, and Puff had already homered in the first game, which we'd lost. He homered again his first time up in the second game, and the next time he came to the plate, he hit a looper off the end of the bat into shallow left field. Only, he almost forgot to run to first, because he was too busy looking at the superballs—those little sparkly rubber balls that'd you'd get from vending machines—that were bouncing around by home plate. He'd broken his bat on the hit, and about five or six of those balls came tumbling out of the top of it!

Oh, we were dying in the dugout! Thurman was all-business during the game, but even he was laughing so hard I thought he was about to fall over. Bill Virdon went out and had a long talk with the umpire, and there was a whole big stink about it. In the end, they called Nettles out, but let his earlier home run stand.

It was a weekend game, and we were in first place at the time, so the Shea clubhouse was filled with writers from every paper in New York, New Jersey, and Connecticut, and they all grilled Nettles about it. He claimed that a fan had given the bat to him as a present, and he had no idea that these balls—which could bounce like 50 feet in the air off of a hard surface—were hidden inside it. I'd heard of corked bats before, but I'd never actually seen one. After that, I started looking at everybody's bats in batting practice, to see if there were any drill holes in them, but I never found one. But we gave Puff a hard time about that for the rest of the season.

The other interesting thing about that series against the Tigers was it was the first time we saw Ron LeFlore. There was a big buzz about him, because he'd been in the penitentiary just a year before, but Billy Martin had heard about what a great ballplayer he was and got the Tigers to give him a tryout. Everybody wanted to see him run, because they'd heard he could really go. Thurman said, "He's not gonna run against me!"

LeFlore did, though—he stole three bases off Thurman in that series, but each time it was close enough that LeFlore didn't try to steal on him too often after that. And now that Thurman knew LeFlore's moves, he could "cheat" a bit and anticipate when he would be running. Thurman could practically snatch the ball off the bat and get it down to second before you knew what even happened. LeFlore took notice—he almost seemed surprised by how quick Thurman's throws had gotten there, and by the third throw he realized that Thurman's delivery wasn't a fluke. He was very careful on the basepaths against us after that.

The Yankees struggled most of the season to get more than a game or two above the .500 mark, but the team caught fire in August and September, launching itself into the heart of a fierce pennant race with the Orioles and Red Sox. It was an exciting time for the team and its fans—especially in mid-September, when the Yankees were actually out in front by a few games. But Ron found himself on the bench for big portions of that stretch. Frustrated by Ron's lack of power production, Virdon had begun using the switch-hitting Roy White as the team's DH against right-handed hitters, while splitting the DH duties against left-handers between Lou Piniella and Alex Johnson.

I usually didn't have big slumps—for me, a bad slump was going like 2-for-15, nothing much worse than that. But on June 5, I went into the game hitting .356, and went 0-for-6 in a 15-inning game. I went into a big slump after that; I wasn't hitting any homers, and my average started creeping down just below .300.

I was hitting the ball well, but it was always finding their gloves. I would be sitting in the clubhouse or on the bus, completely miserable, thinking, "What am I doing wrong? Why am I hitting it right to everyone?" Or things like, "That pitch I struck out on, why did I swing at it? Should I have let it go in that situation?" I'd go off the deep end analyzing it and analyzing it.

Thurman would knew exactly what I was going through, because he was as serious about hitting as I was, and he was having his own difficulties at the plate. He'd tell me, "Stop thinking about it, Bloomie. You're only gonna mess yourself up more. You've got a natural swing and a good eye—put your trust in that, and you'll come around."

He was right, though I couldn't do much to come around when Virdon benched me in August and September. It made no sense to me, as I was still hitting around .300. I mean, how do you bench a .300 hitter? Finally, the last weekend of the season, Virdon put me in the lineup against Gaylord Perry in Cleveland. I always did okay against Gaylord, and I hit two home runs off him to help win the first game of the doubleheader. I was on the bench for the second game, but then I came in as a pinch-hitter and hit another homer to tie up that game. Thurman was like, "I guess all you needed to do was take some swings off Gaylord Perry, and you're back in business!"

Thurman usually did okay against Gaylord, too. Bobby Murcer hated to hit against him, though. Everybody knew Gaylord threw a spitball; he'd go to his cap a hundred times, go to his jersey a hundred times, but if you asked the umpire to go out and check him, they'd never find anything. So I always went up there thinking, "I'm not going to swing at anything around my knees—I'm only going to swing at something up in my chest." Because if it's a spitter, and it's coming in at your knees, it's going to break all the way down in the dirt, and you're going to look like a fool trying to chase it. Bobby couldn't help himself, though; he would always end up chasing it, and he'd come back to the dugout so angry you thought his head was going to explode!

From Cleveland, the Yankees flew to Milwaukee. They were just a game behind the Orioles, with two games left to play, but their pennant chase would come to a premature end in the lobby of Milwaukee's Pfister Hotel.

The Pfister was one of the nicest hotels we'd stay at on the road, a beautiful old place right down by the lake with really nice rooms. But boy did we make a mess out of their lobby that night! What happened was, our plane out of Cleveland was delayed, so everybody was drinking a bit to pass the time, and Rick Dempsey and Bill Sudakis, who was a utility man for us that season, started getting into it for some reason. Bill was not a nice guy, even when he wasn't drinking, but that night he was feeling especially mean. They kept talking smack to each other on the plane, and then on the bus to the hotel, and then… *boom*! It was like a freight train hit that lobby! They went flying onto this beautiful old antique couch and snapped the legs right off of it!

People started piling on, trying to separate them—me, Sparky, Thurman, Bobby, No Neck, we were all trying our best to pull them apart, but they kept rolling around and smashing into tables, knocking lamps onto the floor, it was crazy. And this was like at three in the morning, so the hotel had to call the police, because they didn't have enough security people there to handle it. They called up to Bill Virdon's room, because he'd already checked in and missed the whole brawl. We saw him come out of the elevator, absolutely livid, and Thurman was like, "Hey, Bloomie, we'd better get up to our rooms."

I got up early the next day, and was heading down to get some breakfast when I ran into Elston Howard. Ellie said to me, "George is flying in today for a team meeting about what happened last night. And Bobby has a broken finger." Bobby had been hurt while trying to get ahold of Sudakis, and he couldn't play the remaining games of the season.

All I could say was, "Oh, shit."

With Murcer out of the lineup, the Yankees lost 3–2 to the Brewers in 10 innings, eliminating themselves from the pennant race. They would finish in second place, two games behind the first-place O's, with an 89–73 record, and Bill Virdon would be voted the American League's Manager of the Year.

Ron finished the season with a .311 average, 10 homers, and 48 RBIs in 90 games, while Thurman—who'd caught 137 games despite his nagging hand injury—finished with a .261 average, 13 homers (the second-highest total on the team behind Nettles' 22), and 60 RBIs. Murcer, who led the team with 88 RBIs, hit a career low 10 home runs while batting .274, a 30-point drop from 1973. And just three weeks after the Pfister brawl, the Yankees announced that they were trading him to the San Francisco Giants for Bobby Bonds.

Thurman and I were so shocked when we heard that Bobby had been traded. George had told him that he would be a Yankee forever. Bobby, Thurman, and I were supposed to be the building blocks of another era of Yankee greatness, but now we had to move on without him. Bobby and Thurman were so close, and their wives were so close, too. And ever since I'd come up with the team, Bobby and Thurman had been our leaders, and now it was just Thurman in that role. I knew he could handle it, but I also knew how much we were all going to miss Bobby.

8

Tearing It Up

Though the Yankees had shown remarkable improvement during the second season of the Steinbrenner era, George himself hadn't fared too well in 1974. He was indicted in April on 16 counts of obstructing justice and making illegal contributions to Richard Nixon's 1972 presidential campaign via his company American Shipbuilding. In August, shortly after Nixon had resigned from the presidency in disgrace, he pleaded guilty to two of the counts and was fined $15,000, while American Shipbuilding was fined another $20,000.

Steinbrenner's troubles didn't end there, though; in November, commissioner Bowie Kuhn announced that he was suspending him from baseball for two years. "An essential element of a professional team sport is the public's confidence in its integrity," Kuhn told the press of his decision. "If the public does not believe that a sport is honest, it would be impossible for the sport to succeed."

But Steinbrenner, never one to take a backseat (even when it was mandated by commissioner of baseball), continued to keep one hand on the wheel. Yankees president Gabe Paul, though nominally in charge of running the team, wouldn't (or couldn't) make any major decisions without Steinbrenner's input. And the first major decision the Yankees faced following Steinbrenner's suspension was whether or not to sign 1974 AL Cy Young winner Catfish Hunter as a free agent.

Hunter, who had won 106 regular-season games for the Oakland A's since 1970, and who had helped pitch them to three straight World Series championships, was declared a free agent on December 16, 1974, by arbitrator Peter Seitz, who declared that A's owner Charlie Finley had voided Hunter's contract by neglecting to make a contractually stipulated contribution to Hunter's life insurance annuity. Though Steinbrenner initially balked at the amount of money that would be required to put Hunter in pinstripes, Paul convinced him that the pitcher could take the team back to the postseason. Two weeks after he'd been declared a free agent, Hunter signed a five-year deal with the Yankees for $3.35 million, making him the highest-paid player in major league baseball. He would more than earn his salary in 1975, going 23–14 with a 2.58 ERA and leading the league with a whopping 328 innings pitched and a now almost-unimaginable 30 complete games. Thurman, of course, was behind the plate for most of them.

Thurman was actually a big part of Catfish coming to the Yankees. Thurman didn't do too well at the plate against him, but he always liked him. We got along with a lot of those A's guys, and Catfish was a totally down-to-earth kind of guy in the same way that Thurman was. They used to talk about fishing and outdoors stuff and college football all the time. And of course, Thurman had total respect for him as a pitcher and a competitor; so when he heard that the Yankees were one of the teams talking to him, he called Catfish up a bunch of times and told him, "You've gotta come to New York!" He couldn't wait to catch him.

Catfish had great stuff to begin with—he could throw 95 miles an hour when he wanted to—but he also had incredible pitch placement. I mean, if you put a feather out there for him, he would probably hit it like maybe eight out of 10 times. And he wasn't the kind of guy to dance around the strike zone and run up the count; he would just throw it up there, and if you hit it, you hit it. He made hitters look bad almost effortlessly.

Catfish would always say, "I may give up a home run or two, but I'll beat you 4–3." He would always give up one early, and then he'd settle down. The only time I ever hit a home run off him was in '74; I homered off him at Shea Stadium to tie the game 3–3 in the sixth. I was running around the bases, and he called out to me, "I gave you one, Big Boy! I gave you one, but I'm still going to beat you today!" Well, I came up in the 8th and doubled off him to drive in Bobby Murcer, and we beat him 4–3. But that was his attitude—"I'll give up a home run, but I'll still beat you." And usually, he was right!

Catfish and Thurman made such a great team. Catfish knew everything there was to know about pitching, and Thurman knew everything there was to know about catching. Thurman used to call all the pitches, and I never saw Catfish shake him off once; he and Catfish were always on the same wavelength. To watch Catfish throwing to Thurman, it was like watching Picasso paint.

Thurman was great at doctoring the ball for Catfish, who really knew how to use a scuffed baseball to his advantage. Back then, there was this stuff called Firmgrip, which was this "stickum" type substance that football players like Freddy Biletnikoff used to use. Biletnikoff would always be covered in the stuff; he would hold up one finger, and the football would stick to it! But Thurman was much more subtle about it. He always had a little spot of Firmgrip on the back strap of his catcher's mitt, and he would stick some gravel to it. When he'd catch the ball, he'd quickly scrape it across the back strap of the mitt before throwing it back to the mound, and Thurman's hands were so quick that nobody ever noticed. Using the scuffed baseball, Catfish could make the pitch tail in just a little more on the hitter, just enough that the guy would get jammed. All the pitchers were doing stuff like that back then, though nobody would admit to it. But not everybody could do it like Catfish.

Bobby Bonds, the Yankees' other major acquisition for 1975, brought plenty of power and speed to the leadoff slot, knocking 32 homers and stealing 30 bases, while also showing solid range and glove work in the outfield. Bonds made the AL All-Star team for the only time in his career that season (he'd been to the All-Star Game twice as a Giant), and Thurman and Graig Nettles also made the starting lineup of the Midsummer Classic, the first time that there had been three Yankees in the starting lineup for the AL since 1964.

Bobby Bonds—we called him "BB"—was a great guy, a lot of fun. Bobby and Thurman got along extremely well, because they both liked to joke around and get on people in the clubhouse. Bobby was a real instigator, and when you have Bobby and Thurman together in the locker room or on the bus or the plane, they could really egg each other on to make fun of some of the other guys, and you never knew who they were going to get on. Some guys would get a little riled up by it, but never so upset that they'd crawl over a seat to hit you. I mean, I'd see things like that happen from time to time, but nobody ever went after Thurman or Bobby.

Bobby and Nat got along great, too, and Bobby would often go with us when we'd go down to Nat's office to meet some of the Brunswick artists when they were in town. Bobby loved going to the Apollo with us; it was still the place to go back then, and we saw so many great acts there. We saw Jackie Wilson before he had his stroke, we saw The Dramatics, The Intruders, Curtis Mayfield, Bill Withers, that's what I lived for. To me, you can't find better music than that. We used to go up to the Apollo to see the show, and we'd go eat some soul food over at Sylvia's Restaurant. No Neck Williams, Roy White, and Elston Howard used to join us, too. We had a great time.

There were other nightspots we liked to hit in New York with Nat and his friends. We'd go to Joe Namath's place, Bachelors III, or we'd run into Walt Frazier over at Maxwell's Plum—he had his Rolls-Royce out front with the "Clyde" license plate—or the Marshmallow, which was owned by former Yankee Phil Linz and my friend Art Shamsky from the Mets, or El Vagabondo, where everybody played bocce ball. There's nothing better than New York City when everyone knows you and loves you, and we always had a great time.

Nineteen seventy-five was the year that Nat got in trouble for payola. When he was indicted, the whole thing with guys coming in and out of there all the time with suitcases and big briefcases—I started to understand what was happening a little better. I had no idea what payola was before that. I was naïve. But Thurman and I would still go out to the Stage Deli with him, and sit there with him and Wassel and Soupy Sales, like it was no big deal. I mean, everybody paid to get their records played on the radio, right? Nat didn't seemed bothered by it, and his troubles didn't have anything to do with us, so we weren't bothered either.

Bobby Bonds was a friendly guy, and he was a guy who loved to go out all the time and meet people—and, unfortunately for him, he was also a guy who really loved to drink. That guy was so talented, a true five-tool player, and I have no doubt that he would have been in the Hall of Fame if it wasn't for his drinking. A lot of times when we were on the road, I would kind of be Bobby's minder, because he knew I didn't drink. He would say to me, "Bloomie, I'm going to go to this place tonight. Will you come with me and make sure I'm okay?" He didn't want to take a chance on being somewhere with people he didn't know, and maybe getting in trouble.

I understood what he meant, because the places we used to go on the road weren't always the nicest kind of places. For instance, when we were in Detroit, Bobby loved to go to the Lindell AC and hang out with Earl Wilson, who used to pitch for the Tigers. Earl retired before I had a chance to face him, but he had the biggest hands I'd ever seen, and I heard that he was like the JR Richard before JR Richard.

Earl was always great to us, and the people in Detroit were hip, but when you go into places like that, you know, you don't always know what you'll get. It was dark in there, and we'd always see a fist fight in the parking lot, and sometimes in the bar, too. And a lot of times, we'd be walking back from there to the hotel and Bobby would be laughing and joking and yelling at people, and maybe they wouldn't always get the joke. And Bobby would maybe push somebody once in a while, and I'd have to step in and calm things down. I really liked Bobby, but I didn't always like that part of hanging out with him. But when Bobby would say to me, "You've got to go with me tonight," I couldn't say no. He was a pretty streaky hitter with us, and when he wasn't hitting well, that was when he'd really want to go out and drink away his troubles. And I know he was having a little bit of problems at home, which didn't help.

When you're on the road, you realize that every city has a different feeling and style, different music and—hopefully—a different place you can hang out after the game. We didn't go out in Oakland much; the guys from the A's would tell us, "You don't want to even think about walking around here at night." The only other place we would usually go other than the bar at the Holiday Inn where we would stay when we played the A's was Jack London Square, down by the water.

When we'd play the Rangers in Texas, there was a big disco in Dallas called Elan, which was always where we'd go; they had the girls wearing all the scarves and satin pants, and Donna Summer was always playing when you'd walk in. When we'd play the Angels, we would be stuck in Anaheim where there wasn't much to do, but the Disneyland Hotel had a disco, and we would congregate down there after the game. Kansas City had more of a country and western feel than any other place we played, and Thurman enjoyed that; a lot of the bars had these electric bucking broncos, and Thurman liked to place bets on how long the riders would hang on. Thurman loved to go out after a game and blow off some steam. He left the ballgame at the ballpark better than anyone I ever played with. He might throw his helmet in the dugout or break a bat in the tunnel if he was in a slump; and if Thurman couldn't throw somebody out of the second base, and then they scored to beat us, he'd feel bad for a while. But if you saw him out on the town two hours later, you'd have no idea he'd had a bad game. His attitude was, you play 162 games, and having bad games are just part of being a professional.

Some guys would stay in their rooms, or they'd go somewhere else than we did, but most of us were always going to the same places. Sometimes we'd sit together at a big table and sometimes we would be scattered around the booths or the bar, but we always kept an eye out for each other, just in case there were any problems. Sometimes we'd show up at a place and the bouncer would recognize us and say, "Hey, you need to get your teammate outta here, because he's starting to cause some problems." We'd go in and get him out, before things got heated.

If we went out to a disco, the Black guys on the team were usually the ones who'd get up dance. The White guys? We couldn't dance to save our lives. Thurman, Catfish, and myself, we'd just sit there at the disco and watch everybody. The big dancer on the team was No Neck Williams; he absolutely loved to dance. Alex Johnson was a great dancer. Roy White loved to dance, too, but he wasn't that good. Rudy May, who we got from the Angels in '74, he was a good dancer, but most of the time he'd just sit there and look cool. We called him "the Dude," because of the way he carried himself. There was nobody cooler than the Dude! In '76, when we got Mickey Rivers and Oscar Gamble, those two guys would really love to hit the floor—Oscar even had his own disco down in Montgomery, Alabama.

We tried to stay out of trouble when we went out, especially in New York; because even though we didn't have cell phones and social media back then, being an athlete and living in New York City, people would recognize us and you could end up in the papers. Before George owned the team, it was actually a little bit more lax, because we were just a baseball team to CBS. But when George bought the team, he wanted us to be Yankees at all times.

And it seemed like George watched everybody, all the time. He knew what we were doing at all times, if we were at the ballpark or not. He watched you taking batting practice. He watched to see if you were working hard at your trade. He felt that when you put your Yankee pinstripes on, it meant something. He'd say, "You're part of the Yankee tradition, and that means when you put the uniform on, you've gotta give 120 percent." But Thurman never needed pep-talks like that; he always knew that when you put those pinstripes on, it was sacred, which is why they've never changed them since the days of the original Bronx Bombers.

Even during his suspension, George found ways to keep tabs on us. I remember coming to Shea early one day, and Catfish came in right after me. Catfish was pitching that night, but he'd got there early to do an ad for somebody out on the field. It was maybe noon, and the game wasn't until 8:00. We were standing in front of the dugout, watching the photographer set up his equipment, when suddenly the dugout phone rang. I walked over and picked it up, and it was George. "I need to speak to Catfish," he said. I handed the phone to Catfish, who talked to George for a few seconds before hanging up the phone.

"What did he say?" I asked.

Catfish just laughed and said, "He told me that if I don't win tonight, he's going to fine me."

Some players have favorite ballparks to hit in, but Thurman never really talked about having a particular ballpark that he loved to hit in. Thurman just liked to go out and play. If he had a bad ballgame, he would never blame the ballpark for it, and he hit pretty well in most of the places we played. He even hit well at Shea! The only place I remember him complaining about was the Kingdome in Seattle, when the Mariners joined the American League in '77. But that was understandable. Everybody hated that place.

With Thurman, it really came down more to the pitcher he was facing. Frank Tanana, who really came into his own in '75, used to just kill him; even though Tanana was a lefty, his breaking pitches were so good he always gave Thurman fits. On the other hand, Thurman always liked to hit against Jim Palmer, even though Palmer was a righty and one of the best pitchers in baseball at the time. He always did pretty well against right-handers who would come in over the top like Palmer did. I hit right-handers better than he did, and obviously he hit lefties better than I could, but we both found Palmer very easy to hit. He threw hard, but his ball didn't really have great movement. He had a plus-plus fastball, and a very, very slow curveball; he never threw a hard breaking pitch, and he never threw a slider. And since he came in straight over the top, I could see the ball extremely well. Thurman could see it well, too.

Luis Tiant—now there was a guy both Thurman and I had trouble with. I mean, nobody hit really well off Tiant, as far as I knew. He threw from all different angles, had unbelievable control and could throw any pitch anywhere he wanted to, and his ball moved as well as anybody ever in the game of baseball. He would come at you sidearm, submarine, three-quarters, over the top, and it was so difficult to keep track of the ball before he threw it to you. You'd see his glove, his feet, his knees, and the back of his head before you'd see the ball. With any pitcher you faced, you'd try to time them, but you couldn't do that with Luis; you'd think you had him down pretty good, and then he'd stay on his back foot for an extra second, and that would totally mess up your timing. Sometimes it's fluid, then he throws in one of those little pauses, and once you start timing that up, he speeds up and does like a hop-skip, and he's pitching you real quick. Timing means an awful lot to a hitter, and Luis played hell with it. I know Thurman was very happy when Luis came over to the Yankees in '79. Not only is Luis a prince of a guy, but now Thurman didn't have to face him anymore.

Jim Slaton, who pitched for Milwaukee, was a guy Thurman and I both definitely loved to hit off of. When the Brewers came to Shea Stadium for a series at the end of April, we were both really looking forward to facing him; he was one of those guys that you knew you could get at least a couple of hits off of. Sure enough, in the game he started against us on April 26, I doubled off him in the third to score Bobby, and then Thurman homered off him to score us both. Unfortunately, that was too much for Del Crandall, the Brewers' manager, who yanked Slaton immediately after Thurman's homer. When I came up in the fifth inning, I faced Bill Castro, and I hit a bomb off him that hit the scoreboard—but I immediately fell down, clutching my right shoulder in pain.

I'd been having trouble with pulled muscles, but I'd never felt anything like this before in all my life. I got up and ran around the bases, and by the time I got back to the dugout my shoulder was hurting me so bad, I couldn't even lift up my arm. I fought through the pain for my next two trips to the plate, but as soon as the game was over, Gene Monahan took me to the training room, put some ice on my shoulder, and had the doctor look at it. At that time, nobody had any idea what an MRI was—they just said I had a strain, or I'd probably pulled a muscle in my shoulder. I was in the lineup again the next day, but I could barely swing the bat.

Virdon had me rest for a couple of days, then put me in a couple of times as a pinch-hitter. I got some hits, and felt okay, so he put me back in the lineup as the DH. And then the searing pain kicked in all over again. Now I couldn't even move my shoulder. Dr. Gaynor, the Yankees' team physician at the time, gave me a couple of shots of Butazolidin, which is basically a horse medicine—it's an anti-inflammatory that they used to give to horses at the track when they got hurt— and told me I'd feel better in a couple of days. But my shoulder wasn't getting any better. I hit left-handed, but I throw right-handed, and I still couldn't lob a ball 20 feet. So then they examined me again and determined that it was a muscle tear, and put me on the disabled list for 15 days. And then there was another two weeks on the disabled list, because I still wasn't improving. I was starting to panic, because I hadn't been hitting very well to begin with, and Gabe Paul had already cut my salary because I'd "only" hit .311 in '74 instead of .329 like the year before that.

I was miserable, and felt even worse when I learned that some of the guys on the team thought I was jaking. They wouldn't say it directly, but it would get back to me. Maybe they would say something to a writer, and the writer would say something in the paper about how the guys on the team were looking up to me and they really needed me on the team to win ballgames, and how I need to play even when I'm injured. Thurman came up to me in the training room one day and said, "There's some people on this team saying some shit about you. Just so you know, I stuck up for you, and I don't think those guys are gonna say much of anything about you anymore. And if they do, you need to tell me." I didn't hear anything more after that for a while.

Finally, after a month on the DL, my shoulder loosened up enough that I could swing the bat okay, and Virdon put me back in the lineup. After a rough April and May, we started to get hot in June, and I was excited to contribute again. I was hitting the ball pretty good, but I was hitting with no power at all, no strength in my shoulder. I'm getting base hits, hitting a few doubles, but no home runs; I don't have enough strength in my shoulder to drive the ball out of the park.

We were playing the Twins at Shea Stadium, right before the All-Star break, and I wanted to see if my shoulder was any good. I swung hard at a pitch from Jim Hughes, like a big "for the fences" swing, but I just hit a slow grounder to third and I went down in pain. The Yankees put me on the disabled list again, and I just died inside. To prevent me from injuring it again, the doctors put my arm in a leather brace. They told me I had to leave it on for three weeks and I couldn't shower or bathe while I had it on, which my wife was not too thrilled about. My recovery was slow, and I wound up spending the rest of the season on the DL.

During the ballgames, instead of sitting on the bench, I went up to the press box in my street clothes and watched from there. I wasn't making many trips with the team, but I was still going to every home game. I would take my physical therapy in the trainer's room, and then I'd go up and sit with the writers. I always got along well with most of those guys, so we'd talk—and a lot of times stuff I said would end up in the papers. And the whispers started up again, that I was jaking it, and that I was just having a good time up there talking to the writers. One day, I came into the clubhouse, before almost anybody had got into the ballpark, and on my locker was taped an article from one of the papers calling me the "missing link" of the team. I'm a good-natured guy, but now I'm starting to get really mad. But I can't use my shoulder, so what am I gonna do?

I was out for the rest of the season, and I was miserable. But Thurman was always there, really urging me to keep my spirits up. We'd always sit and eat together before the game, or go into the training facilities and talk. I said to him, "Thurm, I'm really hurting. I'm really, really hurting. And I can't believe that these guys think I'm jaking!"

"I know you're hurting, Bloomie," he said. "But some of these guys, they don't care about anything else except themselves. They're happy to take advantage of you when they wanna go downtown and pick up some clothes or some free food, but they're happy to kick you when you're down. I'm gonna handle this stuff—they're not gonna say anything anymore." And he must have laid down the law, because nothing more was said in '75.

Nineteen seventy-five was where Ron and Thurman's playing fortunes really began to diverge. Between platooning and his injuries, Ron only played in 34 games that season, hitting a career-low .255, with four home runs and 17 RBIs. Thurman, on the other hand, was voted the starting American League catcher in the All-Star Game for the second consecutive year; won his third straight Gold Glove; posted career highs in batting average (.318), runs scored (83), RBIs (102), and total bases (256); and finished seventh in the AL MVP voting.

After going a sizzling 20–9 in June and briefly holding first place in the AL East, the Yankees began to slide back down the division ladder in July. On August 2, with the team two games above .500 and 10 games back in the standings behind the first-place Red Sox, the Yankees fired Bill Virdon. His replacement, Billy Martin, had been fired by the Rangers less than two weeks earlier.

By 1975, the combative Martin had already gained a well-earned reputation for turning losing teams into winners and then completely self-destructing—a pattern he'd established with the Twins, Tigers, and Rangers, the latter of whom had sacked him for punching the team's traveling secretary during a flight. But in the eyes of George Steinbrenner, Martin's fiery spirit and substantial baseball smarts were exactly what the Yankees needed. Martin, a former Yankee infielder (and MVP of the 1953 World Series), wanted nothing more than to don the classic pinstripes again, even if it meant dealing with Steinbrenner's tendency to meddle.

When we first got Billy in '75, I was already on the DL. But he told me, "I can't wait to have you on my team. You're such a great hitter; we always hated to face you!" Thurman really liked it when we got Billy, because he knew Billy had that same kind of winning intensity; Virdon wasn't a bad guy, but he didn't have the same kind of fire in him that Billy had. And Thurman had seen firsthand the difference Billy had made with the Tigers and the Rangers, so he was all for it.

That was also the year Whitey Herzog took over the Kansas City Royals, and they started getting good. Their lineup was packed with good players—George Brett, Hal McRae, John Mayberry, Freddie Patek, Frank White, and Amos Otis—and Whitey had them running like crazy all the time. Billy didn't like a lot of ballplayers on their team, probably from managing against them when he was in Texas, and I remember him flashing Thurman the "knock him down" sign when George

Brett and Amos Otis were at the plate; those were two guys he never wanted to get too comfortable in the batter's box.

Billy knew that our season was already kind of a lost cause when he joined us. He wanted to win every game, of course, but his wheels were already turning for '76. To save wear and tear on Thurman's knees, Billy played Thurman at DH a bunch of times in August and September, while Ed Herrmann or Rick Dempsey caught. He also played Thurman a few games at first, in the outfield, and even once at third base; catching was obviously his first love, but Thurman was such a good athlete that he could play most positions.

The funny thing with Thurman was, even when he was our DH, he would leave the field at the end of the ballgame looking like he'd been in a mudbath. For Thurman, it wasn't a ballgame if he didn't get dirty. "Taking it easy" just wasn't in the guy's vocabulary.

To be honest, Thurman liked to get dirty no matter which sport he was playing. Shortly after the season was over, Thurman, Catfish, Sparky, and myself went up to Syracuse to play a charity golf tournament organized by Tex Simone, who was the president and GM of the Syracuse Chiefs. We didn't bring our own clubs, so they provided us with clubs to play with.

I know this will come as a surprise, but most ballplayers, when they get on a golf cart, they drink quite a bit. We were all in different foursomes with guys who'd paid a lot of money to play with us in the tournament, but we met up on every hole and had a drink. Now, I was never a drinker, so I wasn't trying to keep up with the other three guys, but by the 13th or 14th hole, everyone was getting pretty loose. Thurman was in the foursome right behind me, so I stopped at the tee on the 14th to watch him drive on the 13th, which was a par 3 with a lake you had to hit over to reach the green. Thurman was a really good golfer, at least when he hadn't had a few too many beers, but he hit the ball right into the lake with a big splash.

I thought Thurman would take a mulligan and hit another tee shot, but instead he turned and walked back to the golf cart, which was parked at the top of the hill. He got in and revved it up, then started driving down the hill straight for the water. With a big yell of "Geronimo!" he jumped out of the cart right before it reached the water, and hit the ground with a roll. But the cart just kept on going, right into the middle of a lake, and then slowly sank with his clubs and beers and everything else in it. I couldn't believe what I saw. Thurman's sitting on the ground, watching it disappear into the lake, laughing hysterically, and I'm watching him watch it, and I'm just dying. We laughed about that one for years.

9

So Close, Yet So Far

The Yankees underwent another major overhaul between the 1975 and 1976 seasons. Out went Bobby Bonds and pitchers Doc Medich and Pat Dobson, and in came slugging outfielder Oscar Gamble; AL stolen bases king Mickey Rivers; pitchers Ed Figueroa, Dock Ellis, and Ken Brett; and a promising young second baseman named Willie Randolph. Though the Boston Red Sox, who had taken the Cincinnati Reds to seven games in the 1975 World Series—which many observers were now calling one of the best ever—were widely favored to repeat in the AL East, the Yankees were suddenly looking like a far more intimidating team than the one that had slogged along at a .500 pace for much of the previous season.

After two years in Flushing exile, the Yankees returned to a newly renovated Yankee Stadium in 1976, with George Steinbrenner—his two-year suspension having been cut to one and change by Bowie Kuhn for "good behavior"—returning to the refurbished owner's box. Between the team's colorful new additions (Ellis, Rivers, and Gamble were all larger-than-life characters), Steinbrenner's return, and the first full season of Billy Martin at the helm, the foundations had been firmly laid for the pinstriped circus that would become known as "the Bronx Zoo."

Spring training got off to a late start in 1976. During the winter, Peter Seitz—the same arbitrator who had sprung Catfish Hunter from his A's contract a year earlier—ruled that National League pitchers Dave McNally and Andy Messersmith had, by playing the entire 1975 season without a signed contract, thus earned the right to offer their talents to the highest bidder as free agents. This development, which was supported six weeks later by federal judge John Oliver, essentially nullified MLB's long-standing reserve clause, and sent MLB team owners into a panic. Desperate to put their lucrative genie back in the bottle, the owners locked the players out of camp for two weeks in protest. Commissioner Bowie Kuhn, cognizant of what a massive public relations disaster it would be to shut down the national pastime in the midst of America's Bicentennial celebrations, finally decreed that the camps be opened in the middle of March. Players and owners would finally come to an agreement on free agency in July, establishing an annual free agent re-entry draft for players who'd played a full season without a signed contract. This agreement would have radical long-term effects on the financial future of the game, and would have a profound effect on the Yankees, as well.

Ron arrived at camp from New York City feeling anxious to resume his role as the Yankees' primary left-handed designated hitter. Thurman, who flew from Ohio to Fort Lauderdale, found a new role waiting for him when he arrived: Steinbrenner and Billy had decided to name him team captain, the Yankees' first since Lou Gehrig. He also found a new, two-year, $275,000 contract waiting for him, which made him the second-highest player on the team behind Catfish Hunter.

Thurman seemed almost a little embarrassed when he told me that George and Billy had named him team captain. Billy told Thurman he wanted him to lead the team by example, and he'd already been doing that since 1970. That's just who Thurman was, and he didn't think a title was necessary. He really was the leader of the team, both on the field and in the clubhouse, and not just with the pitchers. He knew how to call a great game, but he also knew how to push the buttons of each and every player on the team to get them to play to the best of their abilities—and if he didn't already know, like with new guys Mickey and Willie, he picked it up quickly. That kind of thing came really naturally to him. He was a natural captain, a natural leader.

Thurman was back in Canton during the off-season, but we talked on the phone all the time. This was when he was really starting to get into buying commercial properties in the Canton area, and he would call up to tell me about his latest investments, and to see how my shoulder was doing. The Yankees had decided I didn't need surgery, so I just did physical therapy and worked my tail off all winter. Now I'm looking like Zeus, and I'm strong as a bull, but I still can't throw a ball at all.

"I'm doing everything I possibly can," I confided to Thurman during one of our calls. "But my right arm is like a noodle. I know that's not what anybody wants to hear, but you're a brother of mine, and I've gotta tell you these things."

"You can talk to me about it any time you want to," he reassured me. "I know you're trying hard to be ready for the season, and I know you'll get there. And don't worry—I'm not gonna tell Billy or anyone else about your arm."

We were already good friends, but in some ways my injuries actually made it more of a close-knit thing, because he became kind of protective of me, and because I knew I could tell Thurman about things I couldn't tell anybody else. The last thing I wanted to do was tell Billy, because he'd dump me from the team in a heartbeat. But Thurman was my leader, my friend, and my confidante, and I could trust him not to tell anybody about it. He really was our captain even before they'd named him the captain.

So I get down to spring training, and I'm still hurting bad; I'm seeing all these different doctors down in Florida and getting all these shots, but it's not really helping. If I'm playing first, and somebody's heading home and I'm supposed to throw the ball home to nail him, there's no way I can make that throw to Thurman; I just can't do it. And when I'm hitting, I still have the ability to hit line drives, and I'm still strong and quick enough to hit some really hard line drives that are going for singles and doubles, but I can't really let loose. When you swing, you really have to follow through, and I just cannot follow through enough to hit the ball over the fence. I can only go about 50 percent or three-quarters of the way around, but that's it. I'm hitting fly balls that would have been 400 feet a year ago, but now they only travel about 350. Even in batting practice, I'm not jacking the ball out anymore. I'm struggling and feeling miserable about it, but I've gotta play. I love baseball, and I want to play. It's what I do, and I don't want to let my teammates down.

The Yankees had picked up Tommy Davis during the off-season. He'd won a pair of batting championships with the Dodgers in the early '60s, and he could still swing the bat, but he'd been hampered for years by leg and foot injuries. Tommy was one of those guys whose career was extended for a few seasons by the DH rule, and Billy's plan going into '76 was that he would be our right-handed DH against lefties, and I would be the left-handed one against righties. But then Tommy didn't hit so well during spring training, and the Yankees released him. I guess Billy figured that Lou Piniella or Roy White could DH from the right side if necessary.

I was hitting pretty well, but without a lot of pop, and Billy noticed. Right at the end of spring training, Billy took me aside and said, "Boomer, we need you to hit home runs. I need you to hit for power."

I said, "Billy, I'm hitting pretty good! I'm having a pretty good spring, and I'm driving in a lot of runs for you!"

He said, "But I need for you to be a power hitter like you have been in the past. We need a DH who can knock it out of the park."

And that's when I thought to myself, "Oh, crap—I've gotta swing hard!"

We're supposed to fly north for a season-opening three-game series in Milwaukee before we head to New York for Opening Day at the new Yankee Stadium. But before we leave, we have to play one last exhibition game against the Mets in Fort Lauderdale. George hates us to lose to the Mets, and I know Billy is watching me closely to see if I can still hit for power, so I just decide to swing for the fences. The second time up, I swing all the way through and hit a shot to right field, but the pain that rips through me is so bad, I can't even run down to first base; honest to god, they actually throw me out at first base from the outfield.

The next thing I know, I'm on the training table in the clubhouse, and George and Gabe Paul are standing over me. "We want to find out what's wrong with your shoulder," George tells me, "so we're going to send you to Dr. Jobe and

Dr. Kerlan down in California. We're gonna fly you outta here on the next plane."

Thurman came into the clubhouse between innings to check on me; he still had his catcher's gear on. "This is really bad, Thurm," I told him. "I don't think I can handle another year like last one."

"Don't think about that," he said. "Just take care of it, and we'll have you back in the lineup with us before you know it."

Billy stopped by, too, but his words weren't so comforting. "You really got me in a tough spot now, Boomer," he yelled at me. "We just got rid of Tommy Davis, and now I'm going into Opening Day without a regular DH!" As if I wasn't feeling bad enough already.

I had to have someone help dress me, and help me get all my stuff from Fort Lauderdale packed up. The team flew me first class to L.A. to meet with Dr. Frank Jobe and Dr. Robert Kerlan, who had helped save Tommy John's career a few years earlier with their experimental ligament surgery. They put a dye in my shoulder—the Yankees' doctors hadn't done that—and they found out that I had a bisected tear in my tendon. My tendon wasn't torn, it was completely split in half. The doctors said they had never seen one as bad as that. They were like, "I can't believe you actually swung the bat!" They made plans to operate on me the next day.

It was a major problem, and I had to be in the hospital for a week. I wanted to at least be back in New York for Opening Day at the new stadium, but that wasn't an option. George called me up after I got out of surgery, and he sounded upbeat. "We heard that they found out what was wrong, and we feel you're gonna come back," he assured me. "We're gonna do everything we can to get you back." Four or five days later, Thurman called me up after he got back to New York. "Gabe Paul told me what was happening with you," he said. "Just get better, my friend. Don't worry about anything else. You're my brother. Just get better."

Thurman had broken a finger towards the end of spring training, and the word as we broke camp was that he was going to DH for the first few weeks of the regular season while he healed up, and that Rick Dempsey would catch. That plan lasted four whole games, and Thurman was back behind the plate for Opening Day at the new Yankee Stadium. "There was no way I was gonna miss that," he laughed when he told me. "Are you kidding?"

When I finally got back to New York and went out to the ballpark, I was stunned. It was so clean, and they'd totally opened it up—all the old pillars and obstructed views were gone. The clubhouse was all cleaned up as well, and they'd replaced the old metal lockers with beautiful wooden ones they'd had made for us. They made the whole place far more comfortable. But even with all the changes and modernizing, it still kept the magic of the old Yankee Stadium. There was nothing in the world like it. I couldn't wait to play there again, even if the "short porch" in right wasn't quite as short as it used to be.

But it would be a while before I could do that. The doctors said I would be out until July or August; the Yankees had to get Carlos May from the White Sox to fill the left-handed DH slot for the time being. No offense to Carlos, but I knew I was a much better hitter than him. For now, all I could do was my physical therapy, which meant showing up early at the ballpark for home games, and traveling with the team on the road, since there would be nobody back at the stadium for me to do therapy with.

When I was traveling with the team, I didn't really feel part of it, even though I would have breakfast every day at the hotel with Thurman and Roy and Mickey, or we'd go out to a little diner nearby if we wanted to get away from the autograph hounds. And then I'd catch the bus to the ballpark with the guys, or I'd go there early with Gene Monahan and get my treatment. Then I'd sit around the clubhouse talking to the players that I wanted to talk to, and watch batting practice from the dugout, but I wasn't allowed to be in the dugout during the game because I wasn't on the active roster. So when the game started I would stay in the locker room and watch the game on TV or listen to it on the radio, or I would go up to the press box and watch the game from there and talk to the writers.

You're part of the team, but you're not part of the team. You're not contributing, and you feel like you're a loose piece of luggage; it wasn't really a fun time, but I had to do it. I tried to get as much treatment in as I possibly could. It was killing me that I couldn't help the team, that I couldn't really be part of the best team I'd ever been on. We were in first place in the division from the third game of the season, and never looked back. But every time Billy Martin came into the trainer's room and asked, "Bloomie, can you play tomorrow?" my heart would just sink.

Then somebody would chime in and say, "He's going to be in here for the rest of the year!" There was always jabbing among ballplayers, but these jabs went a little bit deeper because these were things that I didn't have a comeback for, things that I had no real control over. They're not ragging me for striking out or doing something stupid in the field. Believe me, I would have much rather have done something stupid on the field, because at least I'd be out there playing!

But my arm's still in a sling, I can't do anything, and I'm miserable. I'd pulled some muscles in '74 and had to sit for a bit, I'd missed half of '75 because of my shoulder injury, and here I am in '76, and I'm hurting so bad. And people started talking again, saying that I'm stealing George Steinbrenner's money. I'm only getting paid like $40,000 a year, but back then that's still a good amount of money. I heard little things from the writers, like, "This guy said this about you, this guy said that," and it's killing me.

I told Thurman, "I'm doing everything I possibly can! I want to help this team win the pennant!"

"I know you do, Bloomie, and I know you're working as hard as you can," he reassured me. "Just go do your thing, and don't worry about what people are saying."

I truly appreciated Thurman telling me that, but it was hard to follow his advice, because he always had a much thicker skin than I did. Except for that one time in June, where we were playing the A's at Yankee Stadium, and Thurman overthrew second trying to nail Don Baylor, who then scored to put the A's up 7–6 in the top of the ninth. Thurman then came up in the bottom of the ninth against Rollie Fingers with a chance to tie the game, but he struck out and the Yankees fans booed him. After all he'd done for the team! I couldn't believe it. And then I saw Thurman walking slowly back to the dugout with his hand raised, proudly giving the middle finger to the stands. "Oh no, Thurm, now you've done it," I thought. Knowing what the New York papers were like, I figured they'd never let him forget this.

Of course, when Thurman stepped to the plate the next day, the fans gave him a standing ovation. New York in '76 was a tough town, and Thurman's reaction to the boos had been a typical New Yorker's kind of reaction—"Hey, I'm working hard here, and if you don't like it, go eff yourself!" It made them love him even more, because they realized that he was truly one of them.

A couple of weeks later, Thurman had a collision at the plate with Charlie Spikes of the Indians, which knocked him out of the lineup for a while at the end of June. Charlie Spikes was a huge guy. He was a No. 1 draft pick by the Yankees in '69, and had been a teammate of ours; there was no malice involved with him smashing into Thurman, but he was the kind of guy who would never back down, and Thurman was that kind of guy too. Thurman wasn't angry at Charlie, but he was really frustrated by having to sit on the bench for several days in a row. "How do you do it, Bloomie?" he asked me. He was like a caged tiger, anxiously waiting for his time to break free. I knew the feeling.

George and Gabe pulled off a major trade in June with the Orioles, which sent Rick Dempsey, Tippy Martinez, Rudy May, Scott McGregor, Dave Pagan, and brought us Doyle Alexander, Elrod Hendricks, Kenny Holtzman, and Grant Jackson in return. Kenny was a tough guy, and a really smart one. He was a rep for the Players Association, a total union guy, which is why a lot of front office people didn't like him. But he'd had some great years with Oakland, and the Cubs before that, and Thurman loved catching him. Kenny and Catfish were already friends from their days in Oakland, and like Catfish, Kenny was the loosest guy in the whole world whenever he took the mound. Just give him the ball, and he's ready to go. Kenny and Thurman got along because they always played cards together. Kenny and Catfish and Thurman would play gin in the clubhouse all the time, and Kenny and Catfish would needle each other constantly, but you could tell that they really loved each other.

Billy was unhappy about the big trade, because he hadn't been consulted about it, and because George told him that we were now guaranteed to win the pennant—and that Billy would have no excuse if we didn't. But it turned out to be a great deal for us, because Kenny and Doyle Alexander won 19 games between them, and Grant Jackson won six for us as a reliever and a spot starter. Grant was a really good pitcher, but I knew from watching him with the Orioles that he was the kind of pitcher who, if he gave up a home run or a big hit, would immediately lose his composure. But he and Thurman totally clicked in '76, and Thurman was great about keeping him on track.

My two favorite new additions to the team, though, were Mickey Rivers and Oscar Gamble. Oscar was such a beautiful guy, so sweet and laid-back and always smiling, and always a serious left-handed power threat at the plate. Everybody remembers his gigantic afro, which the Yankees made him trim, but they forget what a great hitter he was, and how far he could drive the ball even with that weird hunched-over stance of his. We'd become friends when he was playing for Cleveland; "The Big O" was from Alabama, and we'd grown up listening to a lot of the same soul music, so we immediately clicked on that level. We used hang out by the batting cage together and watch each other hit, and if I hit a bomb he would tease me saying he could hit it further. "I heard how far you hit that ball off of Nolan," he'd say, talking about a tape-measure homer I hit off Nolan Ryan at the old Yankee Stadium.

"Did anyone see it come down?" I'd reply. "Because if it came down, I didn't get it all!" We'd crack each other up like that. We remained good friends until he passed away.

Mickey was the best leadoff hitter I've ever seen, the fastest guy I ever saw at going from first to third, and one of the best base-stealers, too. He more than lived up to his "Mick the Quick" nickname, even though he always walked like an old man with busted feet. He stole three bases against us in one game in '75, when he was playing for the Angels—though Thurman was playing first base that day, so it wasn't his fault.

Mickey was also one of the funniest, craziest people I'd ever met—a great guy, but you could never understand half of what he was saying. He used to needle everybody; he'd always call Thurman, "You little fat boy!" But Thurman loved him, and he and Thurman made a great pair on the field; it was like Mickey was the captain of the outfield, and Thurman was the captain of the team. With Willie Randolph at second, that gave us three All-Star caliber players up the middle.

Mickey was also the biggest horse guy on our team, even though he didn't really know anything about them. I "saved" his life many times, because he'd always forget which horses he'd bet on, and I'd always tell him when his horse won. He always knew when the races were happening, though, and he'd come running into the clubhouse and ask me, "How did I do?"

Most of the time, I'd tell him, "You don't wanna know!"

But if I told him his horse won, he'd say, "Bloomie, you saved my life!"

Thurman was a good horse guy; he knew what he was doing when he was placing a bet. With Mickey, if it's a horse, he'd pick it. He didn't know anything about the horse; it didn't matter. He always had the sheets showing who's racing at Aqueduct, who's racing at Yonkers, who's racing at The Meadowlands, and he would look at them like he knew what he was doing, but he had no idea. He'd just say, "This horse looks good!" If he was on the field while the race was happening, he'd run straight into the clubhouse as soon as the inning was over to see how he'd done.

If I said, "You hit it, you won 40 dollars," Mickey would be the happiest guy in the world; that was big money back then, especially when he was only betting a couple of dollars.

If I told him his horse lost, he'd just turn around without a word and go back to the dugout. But as soon as the next race happened, he'd be back in the clubhouse. "Bloomie, how did I do?"

Back then, baseball was totally different than it is now. It was all about taking the extra base and getting the guy to third so he could score on a passed ball or a grounder. It was all about putting pressure on the opposing pitcher and fielders. Billy Martin really loved having people steal; his strategy was all about putting constant pressure on the other team with our baserunners and he was great at it. Thurman even stole 14 bases that year, a career high. And we had Mickey Rivers and Willie Randolph at the top of the lineup, two guys who could really run.

In '74, Thurman had hit all over the order, hitting every place but leadoff. But in '75, Virdon hit him cleanup, and he was there for most of the season. In '76, Billy put Chris Chambliss in cleanup, and put Thurman in the third position. When you have guys like Mickey and Willie in the one and two spots, and you're in the third spot, you're gonna come up a lot with guys on base, and Thurman lived to hit with guys on base. He didn't strike out a lot, always made contact. I think that was the best position for him; he'd hit a few home runs, but he could really drive in a ton of runs that way.

Mickey really made the team go, and Thurman really kept the team together. As crazy as that team was, with guys like Mickey, Piniella, Nettles, and Dock Ellis, Thurman kept it balanced and calm. If there was a bad play, or if Billy came running out to kick dirt on an umpire, or Piniella was raising a ruckus, Thurman was always the guy that calmed everybody down on the bench or in the field. There was such a great feeling of chemistry on that '76 team. Even Dock Ellis, who came from the Pirates with a bad reputation, turned out to be a super addition to the team. Dock was such an intense competitor, which made him a good match for Thurman and Billy, and he won 17 games for us that year.

Thurman took his captain status seriously, even easing up a bit when writers wanted to talk to him—at least the ones who didn't always get on him and stab him in his back in the papers. The big guys like Dick Young, Red Foley, Maury Allen, Jim Ogle, and Moss Klein, he would be civil with them most of the time and give them what they needed; he might not always be very pleasant about it, but he would talk to them. The other guys, the ones who were just digging for dirt, he would only give one-word answers to, if that. He was never nice to those guys. "Did you do this?"

"Yes."

"Can you elaborate?"

"No."

Billy was a brilliant manager, but he was... difficult. Whenever we played in Cleveland, Thurman would go back to Canton after the game to be with Diana and Tote and the kids, while the rest of us looked for something to do. The only good place to eat near the ballpark was the Theatrical. The owner, Mushy Wexler, was a good friend of Nat's; he knew all the "people" in Cleveland that Nat knew, if you know what I mean. And the guy who loved to eat there more than anybody was Billy. He'd go there to eat every night. They did have great food there, but most of the guys on the team would get up and leave when they saw Billy coming in, or turn around and go somewhere else if they saw he was already at the bar, because when Billy had a few drinks, you had no idea what he was going to say or do.

The Lindell AC had been Billy's favorite place to drink when he'd managed the Detroit Tigers, and whenever we played in Detroit you could find him there after a game.

You'd see him get on the team bus the next morning wearing sunglasses, even though it was cloudy outside, and you knew he'd had a tough evening there.

The visitors' clubhouse at Tiger Stadium was basically just a really big room. It was not air-conditioned at all, but they had these giant, 100-year-old fans hanging from the ceiling, and they'd all be going constantly, and they had these big leaded industrial windows that they'd pull open from the top with a pulley, so all you could see is the sky. Even with the windows open and the fans going, it would be hot as anything in there. The training room was small and you really didn't want to be in it, and there was a tiny room for the manager's "office." The coaches had to dress with the players.

This one morning in Detroit, Billy gets off the bus and goes straight into the manager's office in the clubhouse. He's wearing sunglasses, wobbling, and not talking to anybody. Thurman looks at me and shakes his head. "Billy's not in good shape," he says, and I have to agree. He looks especially rough, even by Billy's standards.

An hour or so later, I'm sitting on the bench watching the guys take batting practice, when Billy shows up in the dugout. He sits down, and the bench there is really small so we're sitting like six inches away from each other, but he doesn't say anything. Finally, right before Billy goes out to home plate to hand the umpires the lineup card, he turns to Dick Howser and says, "You're gonna have to manage this one." Howser is our third-base coach, but today he's going to have to manage the game.

So Billy goes wobbling out to home plate, and Howser turns to us and goes, "Watch this." And right off the bat, Billy starts in on Jerry Neudecker, the umpire, calling him every name in the book. Jerry's kind of taken aback, but doesn't say anything. Finally Billy goes, "Throw me out, Jerry! I can't stand it any longer!" So Jerry tosses him, and the crowd goes wild—Billy's been thrown out of the game before the game's even started! And our old skipper Ralph Houk, who's now managing the Tigers, just stands there watching the whole thing and laughing. When the game starts, I go back into the clubhouse, and Billy is already long gone—probably back to the Lindell AC for a little hair of the dog.

It was September before I finally got the doctors' go-ahead to play. It was too late for me to make the postseason roster, but Billy asked me to dress out, and I was more than happy to put on my pinstripes again after so many months away. I only played once, on September 8, as a pinch-hitter for our DH, Cesar Tovar, who the Yankees had signed a week earlier. We were already up 6–0 against the Brewers when I stepped up to the plate in the sixth against Moose Haas, and then I stayed in the game against Kevin Kobel in the eighth.

I got a big cheer from the fans both times I came up to bat, and it was nice to finally be playing again at Yankee Stadium for the first time in three years, but I really wasn't ready. We already had the game in the bag at that point—Thurman drove in a couple of runs that night, Ed Figueroa pitched a three-hit shutout, and we beat them 8–0—but I still would have loved nothing more than to knock a hit or two. Those guys were usually great pitchers to hit off of, too, but that night I couldn't do anything against them. And when you've been hitting shots off these guys all along, and then you barely put the ball in play against them, you worry that it's time to be put out to pasture. But I still hoped that, if I worked hard enough over the winter with my rehab, I'd be back in the regular lineup in '77.

On September 25, the Yankees clinched the AL East for the first time since the American League had been split into two divisions. It was the team's first pennant since 1964, ending the longest postseason drought in Yankees history. The team's appearance in the playoffs—where they beat the Royals three games to two, winning it all on Chris Chambliss' dramatic ninth-inning home run in Game 5—and the subsequent World Series was a huge morale boost for a city whose severe fiscal crisis had made international headlines just a year earlier. (Most infamously with "Ford To City: Drop Dead," the New

York Daily News' *pithy summation of president Gerald Ford's promise to veto any federal bailout for NYC.) Though regularly characterized in the national media as a brutal and decaying city where mortal danger lurked around every corner, New York was actually in the midst of a vibrant cultural renaissance, and the Yankees' return to the World Series seemed one more indication that the Big Apple was back, baby.*

Unfortunately, the Yankees themselves appeared not quite ready for baseball's biggest stage. Physically and emotionally exhausted from beating the Royals, they barely put up a fight against the rested and loaded Cincinnati Reds, who swept them easily in four games. Thurman didn't go down quietly, though; after going 10-for-23 in the playoffs with two doubles, three runs scored, and another three driven in, he went 9-for-17 against the Big Red Machine with two runs and two RBIs. Thurman's .529 average for the Series was bested only by Reds catcher Johnny Bench, who hit .533, and whose two home runs in Game 4 iced the championship for Cincinnati and earned him the Series' MVP Award.

Watching the two great catchers perform at the peak of their powers was probably the most exciting thing about the otherwise-dull Fall Classic, but when a sportswriter asked Sparky Anderson to compare the two players, the Reds manager made an enemy for life with his answer. "Munson is an outstanding ballplayer and he would hit .300 in the National League, but you don't ever compare anybody to Johnny Bench. Don't never embarrass nobody by comparing them to Johnny Bench."

Johnny Bench was always in the other league, so Thurman didn't get compared to him that much in the press—it was always about him and Carlton Fisk. But the things Sparky Anderson said after the World Series, boy did that make Thurman mad. Sparky later apologized, but I don't think Thurman ever forgave him.

Bench could hit for more power, and he had a better arm, but I never saw a better all-around catcher than Thurman, and nobody was better at working with and controlling pitchers. Johnny Bench and Carlton Fisk, as great as they were, they couldn't call the game the way that Thurman did. You didn't really even need a pitching coach when you had Thurman. Whether it was a rookie or an aging veteran, Thurman could get the best out of these guys. And I can't think of another catcher we played against who could hold his jock when it came to leadership.

I was so proud of Thurman that October, both as a friend and a fan. But it was so hard for me to watch those games. Every baseball player, from the time he's a little kid, dreams of playing in the World Series. Thurman's dream had finally come true; like him, most of the guys on our team—with a few exceptions like Catfish, Kenny, and Dock—had never been there before. Roy White had been on the team since '65, and he was finally getting to live the dream. I was so happy for all of them, but also so depressed because I couldn't truly be there with them. This was my dream, too.

Adding insult to injury, '76 was the first time they ever used the DH in the World Series. If we'd made it a year earlier, I might not have gotten into a game except as a pinch-hitter. But the Reds threw two right-handers at us, Pat Zachry in Game 3 and Gary Nolan in Game 4, and it should have been me in the lineup against them, instead of Carlos May. In Game 3, Dan Driessen of the Reds became the first DH to hit a World Series homer. Maybe that could have been me, if I'd been able to play? Maybe I could have even helped the team win a game, to keep us from getting swept like that? These were the kinds of thoughts that were going through my mind. It was a great team in '76, but it was obvious from the World Series that we were a few pieces short of being able to go all the way.

On November 16, the Baseball Writers' Association of America voted Thurman the American League's Most Valuable Player in a landslide, with the Yankee captain snagging 18 of 24 first-place votes and a 90 percent vote share. It was the first time since Elston Howard had won it in 1963 that a Yankee (or an American League catcher) had been thusly honored. It was well-deserved; Thurman had turned in one of his best seasons at the plate, batting .302 with 27 doubles, 17 home runs, and 105 RBIs in 665 plate appearances, while only striking out 38 times. Though his hand injuries had resulted in a sub-par year defensively, his obvious leadership role with the ascendant Yankees more than made up for it in the eyes of the voters. "It's been a fantastic year, starting by my being named captain of the team at the beginning of the season," he told the press in what was for him an uncharacteristically effusive press conference. "The award tops it all off. It's a great feeling." When asked about the outcome of the recent World Series, Thurman said, "We got beat by a great ball club. We'll be back next year."

Less than two weeks later, Thurman would be back on a press conference podium, this time to welcome Reggie Jackson to the Yankees. One of the most sought-after names in the free agent re-entry draft of 1976, Jackson had been a star with the Oakland A's in the first half of the decade, but A's owner Charlie Finley had traded him to the Orioles in April when it became clear that Jackson intended to play out his option that season. Jackson had made it plain in many interviews during the season that he was only interested in signing with competitive teams in major cities, and the AL champion Yankees fit his criteria perfectly. So, too, did George Steinbrenner's offer of a five-year contract at $3 million.

Billy Martin was not in favor of the Jackson signing, believing that A's outfielder Joe Rudi—also a free agent— would be a better fit for the team. But Steinbrenner overruled him, correctly noting that while Rudi was an excellent player, Jackson was the kind of high-wattage star who would "put butts in the seats" and continue to keep the city's media spotlight fully fixed on the Yankees. Thurman encouraged Steinbrenner to sign Jackson, both out of respect for his abilities—Jackson, after all, had played a major role in getting the A's to three straight World Series—and out of self-interest. Thurman believed that Steinbrenner had assured him that, as captain, he would always be the highest-paid player on the team (save for Catfish, who was a special case). Therefore, he anticipated receiving a raise for the 1977 season commensurate to what Jackson would be making.

Thurman had such a great year in '76. He'd been named team captain, we won the pennant, he won the MVP, and I was so proud of him. This is my brother, you know? We've been through so much together, I've seen what an amazing player and person he is, and now he's finally getting his due as one of the best in the game—and from the press, no less!

But it only took a week for the New York press to stop talking about Thurman and start talking about Reggie, and whether or not he'd come to New York. Before the deal was officially announced, Marty Appel called me up and said, "We got Reggie Jackson!"

"Oh, that's great!" I said.

"Well, I don't know how great it is," he said. "It's gonna cause some friction on our team."

It's true—we'd heard from Catfish and Kenny, who had played with him in Oakland, that he'd caused some problems on the team, both on and off the field. But George didn't care about that; George wanted Reggie because of his home runs, and because he was such an extroverted guy and had such star quality.

Thurman called me from Canton. "They're flying me to New York for this press conference, and they want me to say a few words about Reggie," he said, and we made plans to meet up for a meal when it was all over. So they had the press conference, but when I saw Thurman later he looked glum. "You wouldn't believe this guy that we're gonna have on our team," he said. "I can already tell I'm gonna have problems with him."

"Thurm, what do you mean?" I asked him.

"This guy is so outspoken, and he's going to try to put all the emphasis on him when he comes to our team. He told everybody at the press conference that we were gonna win a lot more ballgames now that he's here. We just won 97 games. C'mon, Bloomie—who does this guy think he is?"

We would find out in just a few months.

10

The Straw That Really Stirred the Drink

It's early in the afternoon of October 18, 1977, and I'm sitting in the whirlpool in the trainers' room at Yankee Stadium, listening to my teammates joking and laughing with each other as they come into the clubhouse. Two days ago, the Dodgers crushed us 10–4 in Game 5 of the World Series, but you wouldn't know it from the way these guys are carrying on.

You couldn't find a major league clubhouse looser than this one. Even with all the characters and personalities on this team, all the drama we'd gone through this season with George and Billy and Reggie, and all the pressure that comes with playing in the postseason, you can't feel any tension or tightness in the air. Thurman's sitting here with me in the trainer's room, relaxing by paging through the *Wall Street Journal*. By this time, our captain already knows exactly how he's going to call the pitches to Ron Cey, Steve Garvey, and the rest of those guys in the Dodger lineup; there are no scouting reports to study, no game plan to go over with Mike Torrez, who's taking the mound for us tonight. Thurman is ready.

From my seat in the whirlpool, I can hear Mickey Rivers and Graig Nettles cracking the other guys up with their smack talk, and I can feel the excitement and electricity vibrating throughout the clubhouse. This is what you work for, to be within one game of winning the World Series. Some guys can't handle the postseason pressure, but *everybody* on this team wants to be at the plate with the game on the line. Thurman, Mickey, Nettles, Reggie, Lou Piniella, Willie Randolph, Chris Chambliss, Roy White, Bucky Dent… they all want to be that guy, and that's part of what makes this team so great.

Cliff Johnson, our backup catcher, wants to be that guy, too, and I can hear him grumbling to somebody in the next room about how little playing time he's gotten in the Series. Cliff is the strongest man in baseball; he always comes to play and you won't find a finer person. But since the current agreement between the AL and NL owners says that the DH can only be used in the World Series during even-numbered years, he'll only get into the game tonight as a pinch-hitter or a late-inning defensive replacement.

I feel bad for Cliff, but I would also give anything right now to even be in his position. Because at least Cliff can still put on his pinstripes, and can still go sit in the dugout with the rest of the team; at least there's still a chance that he can get into the game tonight and make some kind of contribution. Me, I'm still on the Yankees' roster, like I have been since June '71, but there's a "DL" next to my name. I already know I won't be dressing for tonight's game, or be doing anything to help my brothers try to bring the World Series trophy home to the Bronx for the first time since '62. And it's absolutely killing me.

Everything had been going so well for me in spring training. After what was basically a year-and-a-half layoff, my shoulder was feeling great again, I had my full strength back, and I was hitting the ball harder than I had in years. I was hitting doubles, hitting homers, driving in runs. During one exhibition game, I hit a ball over the lights in right field at Little Yankee Stadium, probably a 475-foot shot, and everybody went nuts. The writers saw my power coming back, and suddenly there were all these "Boomer's Back!" stories in the papers.

I knew this was going to be an even better team than the one that made it to the World Series the year before, only to get swept by the Reds. Most of the main guys from '76 were back, and now we also had Reggie, Don Gullett (who George signed as a free agent after he beat us in Game 1 last year), and a scrawny rookie lefty named Ron Guidry, who looked like he was really going to be something special. This team was loaded, Billy Martin seemed to love me again, and everything was super. I couldn't wait for the season to start.

Reggie's arrival had given the Yankees a surplus of left-handed hitters who could serve as a DH against right-handed pitching, including Oscar Gamble and Carlos May. Over the winter, George had been pretty cagey with the press about my status on the team, so I knew I had to give 120 percent in spring training, and prove to him that I still belonged in pinstripes.

Our rivalry with the Red Sox was always intense, even in spring training, and George made it clear to Billy that he wanted us to win all our exhibition games against them. On March 30, just a few days before we were due to break camp and go north for the season, we went to play the Red Sox at their ballpark in Winter Haven. For some reason, Billy decided to make Reggie our designated hitter for that game, and put me in left field, Carlos in right, and Roy White in center. This didn't exactly give us a Gold Glove outfield, but it did stack our lineup with left-handed hitters against Fergie Jenkins, who was starting the game. I'd only ever played a couple of major league games in left field, but I wasn't going to complain. I was feeling great, I was happy to be in the lineup again, and I was determined to do whatever I could to help beat the Red Sox.

In the first inning, I made a throwing error that let in a Red Sox run, but I soon got it back with an RBI single off Fergie. We were up 6–2 in the bottom of the fourth, with Dock Ellis on the mound for us, when Red Sox second baseman Doug Griffin ripped a line drive over my head. Griffin wasn't anybody's idea of a slugger, so we weren't playing him particularly deep, and we weren't playing him to pull. But he really smoked this one, and it was tailing away from me, and I was running and running and running trying to catch up with it...

You've seen that old clip of the minor league outfielder running right through the fence while chasing a ball? Well, that was me hitting the wall—except this was the kind of wall you couldn't run through. The outfield walls at Chain O' Lakes Park were made of concrete cinderblocks, which were like two feet deep, and there wasn't much of a warning track to speak of. Just the year before in spring training, Gary Carter ran into the wall in Winter Haven while playing in the outfield, and had to get about 60 stitches in his head. After that, the Expos had to put him back behind the plate for his own safety.

Gary went on to enjoy a Hall of Fame career after that, but I wasn't so lucky. I hit the wall full-force. I'm lucky I didn't crack my skull. I mean, I could have, because my sunglasses were shattered and my nose was bleeding, but I guess my head didn't hit the wall squarely because my knee hit it first. I don't know if I blacked out or not, but the next thing I know I see Reggie looking down at me, asking "Are you okay?"

Billy, Gene Monahan, Herm Schneider, the whole team— they all ran out to where I'd fallen, to see if I was still alive. "Damn, Bloomie," said Thurman when he reached me, "that's the hardest I've ever seen anyone hit a wall!" He was trying to make me laugh, because he could see I was really struggling. I was covered in blood, and you could see the bones in my knee sticking out through the skin. I was a mess.

It was a long and miserable bus ride back to Fort Lauderdale. I had my leg up, with a bag of ice on my knee, but I knew this was bad. Dr. Danny Kanell met us at Little Yankee Stadium and took me to Holy Cross Hospital. After examining me, he told me that I'd torn my knee tendons, torn my meniscus, torn my ligaments, and completely shattered my kneecap.

I didn't even know what to say. I couldn't believe it. I'd worked my tail off to finally come all the way back from my shoulder injury—but before we'd even broken camp, I was back on the DL with a shattered knee. George flew me up to New York on his plane, and the Yankees scheduled me for an operation at Lenox Hill Hospital with Dr. James Nicholas, who had previously worked on Joe Namath's knees.

While I was waiting to go under the knife, George surprised everyone by trading Oscar Gamble to the White Sox for Bucky Dent, right before the regular season began. Oscar had been holding out for more money, and George had wanted Bucky for years, so the deal made sense to everyone—except for Billy, that is. The arrival of Bucky meant that Fred Stanley, one of Billy's favorites, would lose his starting job at shortstop. And Oscar's departure, combined with my knee injury, meant that Carlos May was suddenly his only left-handed DH option. I'd known Carlos since '68, when we played against each other in the Carolina League, and he was a good ballplayer, but he wasn't the hitter I was. I knew Billy knew that, too—but I didn't expect him to tear into me about it.

"I can't believe what you did to me!" Billy screamed at me, when I walked into the clubhouse on crutches for the first time since my surgery. "You run into an effing wall—now you're out for the season, and we don't have a left-handed DH. You put me in a terrible position!" And then he stormed off.

Thurman was with me and heard the whole thing; he couldn't believe it. "Bloomie, you're gonna make it through," he told me. "I'm gonna push you, if I have to. You're gonna get that knee better. You came back this spring; you were hitting the ball hard, hitting home runs. You're gonna be back."

It was all so strange. Exactly a year ago, Billy had given me the same lecture when I tore my shoulder in the last game of spring training, and Thurman had given me a similar pep talk after my surgery. Like Yogi Berra used to say, it was déjà vu all over again.

It had been a rough spring for Thurman, too, but in a much different way. In '76, after George and Billy had officially named Thurman team captain, George made a verbal agreement with Thurman that he would always be the highest-paid Yankee player, other than Catfish. So when Reggie signed his big free agent deal with George in November '76, Thurman—who certainly deserved a raise for leading the Yankees to the World

Series and winning the AL MVP Award—figured his salary would be bumped accordingly. Unfortunately, every time he tried to broach the subject with George, he got nowhere.

Reggie's me-me-me behavior, of course, only made matters worse. From the moment Reggie arrived in spring training, Reggie was acting like it was all "Reggie or nothing." He kept telling everybody about all the money he was making and all the cars he was driving. We would get him back by charging all sorts of meals and drinks to his hotel room. Every morning, we'd see him down at the front desk, arguing with the clerk about the charges on his account. "How could I possibly have run up a thousand-dollar room service bill?" he would yell, as we all cracked up.

One day during spring training, we were going to West Palm Beach to play the Braves. Everybody gets on the bus—we're taking two buses, because there are a lot of rookies and young players still with the team at that point. This is maybe our third or fourth game of spring training, but it's our first road trip. Billy gets on the bus, Ellie and Dick Howser are there, and everybody's looking for Reggie, because he's not on the bus. Billy says, "Where's Reggie? He's supposed to make this road trip!" The stars and the regular starters don't always make the road trips, but this time everybody was supposed to go up to West Palm.

Reggie pulls up alongside the bus in his rented convertible, with his gorgeous blond girlfriend in the passenger's seat. Somebody yelled, "Reggie, are you coming with us?"

"No," he said, "I got permission from George, I can drive my own car up there."

Oh, that didn't sit well at all. I could tell Billy wanted to say something, but he kept his mouth shut. But we're all going nuts. We're taking the bus to West Palm, and Reggie is directly behind us with his girlfriend, following the bus. We pull up about an hour later in front of West Palm Beach Municipal Stadium, a nice little ballpark. Our bus pulls up where the other buses do, and lets us out, but Reggie doesn't follow us— Reggie pulls up into the players' parking lot and walks to the stadium with his girlfriend. And as soon as Reggie gets out of his car, there are writers there who are waiting to talk to him.

Thurman was a guy who was not afraid to state his opinion. Sparky was a guy like that, too—as were Nettles and Piniella and Mickey—and on the way back to Fort Lauderdale, everybody's grouchy and cursing Reggie out. It was a hot day, about 90 degrees, and we're all hot coming back on the bus, and there's Reggie driving his air-conditioned car back to camp. We pull into the parking lot of Little Yankee Stadium, and everybody immediately smells smoke—while we were gone, somebody had taken all of Reggie's street clothes out of his locker and burned them in the middle of the clubhouse.

Nobody would ever say anything, and it couldn't have been any of us who actually did it, but someone had clearly called up the clubhouse from a pay phone in West Palm and told one of the clubbies to do it. Reggie came in a few minutes behind us, and all the clothes he'd worn to the ballpark were totally burned in the middle of the locker room. I'm never gonna forget that. You should have seen his face when he came in. He started going nuts. He didn't say, "You did it, you did it, you did it," or anything like that, but he said, "When I find out who did this, I'm gonna really get 'em. I'm gonna kill 'em!" But nobody said anything. To this day, nobody has ever fessed up. Thurman definitely got a kick out of it, though.

Most days, as soon as Reggie would come into the clubhouse, he would be swarmed by like 15 reporters. The press loved Reggie because he always had things to say, things that they could write an article about, and Reggie loved the press because he always liked to have an audience. He wasn't the type of guy who could ever just sit there by himself or quietly go about his business; whenever he entered a room, everybody had to know that he was there. And the writers ate that up. Writers don't want somebody low-key, they want somebody who'll stir things up and sell papers, and that was definitely Reggie. Whereas Thurman, they knew he would bite their heads off if they asked him anything.

And then that *Sport* magazine profile came out, with Reggie's infamous quotes about how he was "the straw that stirs the drink," and how Thurman "can only stir it bad," which really angered Thurman. It wasn't like Thurman was jealous of all the attention Reggie was getting—Reggie loved to hold court with reporters, and Thurman would rather have dental surgery than be interviewed—but he was extremely upset about being disrespected, both by Reggie and, he felt, by George.

Reggie was a great player, no question—he'd been an MVP, as well as a big part of a team that had won three straight World Series and five straight AL West titles. And Thurman genuinely respected what he'd done in Oakland. But even with all that, you don't come to a team like the Yankees, a team where the captain is the reigning MVP, and tell everybody that it's your team now. That's not gonna go over too well.

Reggie and I always got along extremely well. And there was never any pressure from Thurman for me to take sides; he made it clear to me that what was going on was between him and Reggie, and him and George. But he was really hurt. Because here's a guy that had been with the organization since '68, he's given 10 years of his life, everything he had, every single day to the Yankees. Here's a guy who's the captain of the team, who just won the MVP, and he's just been thrown under the bus. "I don't get it, Bloomie," he told me one night. "I feel like I've been passed over."

The thing was, we all knew that there was no way in the world we could win without Thurman. He was the catalyst of the team as well as our captain; on and off the field, he created success. And to his credit, even after his falling out with Reggie, and even as mad as he was at George, he never let it hurt his playing, and he never let it hurt his teammates. Because it was of the utmost importance to Thurman that the team was on the right track, even when all the stuff with

Billy and George and Reggie was going on. It was a matter of professional pride to him, even when wiseasses like Nettles, Piniella, and Tidrow would try and get under his skin after games by saying, "Hey, Thurm—you didn't stir the drink well enough today!" You could see the veins bulging out in his neck whenever they said things like that, which was a sure sign that you didn't want to mess with him any further.

Between George and Billy and Reggie and Thurman and Nettles and Mickey, there was a lot of tension on that team. George was always having a big talk with Billy, and then a big talk with Reggie. There were problems after problems. I remember one fight Mickey had with Reggie: Mickey was on the training table, because he didn't feel good that day. Reggie came in, like three hours before game time, and started messing with Mickey. Mickey had turned the lights off in the training room so he could get some rest, but Reggie came in and turned the lights on. Mickey said, "Reggie, turn the lights off—I'm sleeping!" Reggie didn't do it, so Mickey got up and turned them off, and then Reggie turned them on right after he laid down again, and this went back and forth until Mickey finally jumped up and slammed Reggie up against the wall. Guidry got in the middle of it, trying to separate them, and Mickey kept screaming, "I'm gonna kill this motherfucker!" The training room got completely torn up; they knocked the table over, scattered medications all over the floor. It looked like a tornado had hit the place. And that was just your average day in the Bronx Zoo.

George put a lot of pressure on Thurman that year. Thurman was of course the team captain, and George used to bypass Billy and go directly to Thurman and say things like, "This problem better be fixed, or there's gonna be more problems." There was tension there the whole season, and George would always involve him somehow. And that was the time when George really put a lot of pressure on Billy. The phone in the dugout was ringing all the time, to the point where no one would answer it anymore. George put a phone in the owner's box that went directly to Billy in the dugout; there were other phones in there that went to the bullpen, and up to the press box. George used to call up Billy and Thurman all the time when they were on the road, too—Thurman told me he would go down to the hotel coffee shop at seven in the morning, just to get away from George's phone calls.

And the thing was, we were winning games. We had chemistry when we played baseball. It wasn't like we necessarily had the best players in the league, but we played baseball together better than anyone. And you had Thurman out there, working with Guidry, Catfish, Sparky, and all these other great pitchers, and he had all these guys *memorized*. These pitchers loved to throw to him. If Catfish was having a tough outing, Thurman would go out and say some crazy stuff to him like, "You stink today—let's get through this inning and we'll pull you out."

He worked really well with Guidry, who Billy had no confidence in at first because he was so small and wiry. In

June, he was pitching a shutout against the Royals going into the ninth, and Billy started making like he was about to take him out, because he didn't trust Gator yet to go the full nine. Thurman got to the mound first and told Gator, "You better say something to Billy, or he's never gonna let you finish a ballgame."

So when Billy went out and asked him how he was doing, Gator said, "Get your ass off my mound and let me finish the game!" And that was good enough for Billy!

It's true that Reggie really sparked that '77 team when we needed him to. For whatever reason, he was made for the big moment. He lived to come up to the plate in a critical situation, and he always seemed to come up with that big hit at the right time. But it was Thurman who kept that '77 team rolling from day to day. Maybe he didn't have Reggie's flair, but when Thurman talked, people listened. Thurman was a dirty player—not that he was a cheater, but he literally wanted to get his nose in the dirt, get down in the engine room and take control of the situation. He was a George Patton. He made the team go. Whatever Reggie thought, Thurman really was the straw that stirred the Yankees' drink. You don't have many players who have that kind of ability to command the attention and respect of everybody on the team. But Thurman had that.

He also had my back, all through what turned out to be the toughest year of my life. It's easy to support somebody when everything's going great for them. But when you're on the disabled list for a couple of years, and you can't perform up to your team's or your own expectations, or even dress out and sit on the bench… Thurman knew what I was going through, and he knew how much it had to hurt. And even with all of his responsibilities, all the games he had to prepare for and play in, and all the characters and distractions of the Bronx Zoo, his support for me never wavered for a second.

Even though I was on the disabled list, the Yankees made it mandatory that I would go to the ballpark every day to get physical therapy. I would usually arrive at 11:00 on the morning of a night game, when nobody was there except for the clubhouse boys shining shoes and putting the clean uniforms up in the lockers. I was there every single day with Gene Monahan, doing my exercises, and every single day the doctors would work on me for two hours, checking out my knee, checking out my shoulder. I felt like Frankenstein. I was still on the payroll, and I was doing everything I possibly could to get better. But I was miserable. I was the most depressed person in the whole world.

And then when I would be leaving the clubhouse after my treatment, all the other players would be coming in. I'd be getting dressed, and they'd be getting ready to play the game. It was like, "What do I do with myself now?" I didn't feel right hanging around the clubhouse; I felt like an outcast. I'd go out and sit on the bench and watch batting practice, but people would move away from me, like I was a bad omen. Nobody wanted to be around me, because here I am, injured again, and they were afraid my bad luck would rub off on them. I felt completely useless.

Nobody ever came up to me and said, "You're jaking!" But you start to see little things in the clubhouse, and you hear people talking, saying things like, "Well, if we had Blomberg, but who knows if he'll ever play again…"

Billy would look over at me and sneer, "When are *you* coming back?"

I'd say, "I'll be back!" But it was little things, little digs, and it gets to you.

As in '76, I would often go up to the press box to watch the games. But it got to the point where I just couldn't even do that anymore. I'd be up there with all the reporters and writers, with the AP and UPI machines going, I would just be watching the ballgame, but they'd be talking to me, and sometimes even writing stories about what I was saying, and then the next day, there'd be a big story about me in one of the papers—even though I hadn't done anything on the field that day. It was killing me to watch these guys doing so well, game after game. Some of the guys I'd been on the field with for my entire career, guys I'd fight for, but I knew that I couldn't be out there with them.

There's been a lot of great teams in Yankee history, but I don't think there's ever been a team like the '77 Yankees, where the team wasn't just strong, but also so colorful, so full of great personalities. Maybe the closest thing to it was the '72–74

Oakland A's—who, not coincidentally, also had Reggie and Catfish—but even they weren't as strong as we were all the way through the lineup, or in the field. And if I hadn't run into that wall in Winter Haven, I would have fit right in there with them. I'm not gonna brag, but I don't think any of the guys they had DHing on that '77 team were the hitter I was when I was healthy. Is it wrong to say that? Because that's how I felt. I loved competition, and I still believed in myself, that nobody could out-hit me. My career batting average was .302 at that point, and I hit even better than that with runners in scoring position. There was no doubt in my mind that I would have been the DH of the '77 Yankees, and maybe even played a bit of first base. But it wasn't to be.

Even though I wasn't playing, I was still getting a lot of fan mail, letters and postcards wishing me good luck, hoping I'd be playing again soon. My locker was my office, and I'd sit down there every single day signing baseballs, autographs. Each day, I'd probably have 150, 200 autograph requests sent down to me from the mailroom. I'd be sitting down there in the clubhouse, and all these writers like Dick Young, Maury Allen, Red Foley, and Phil Pepe would be talking to me and asking me questions, even though I hadn't really played in two years outside of spring training. I wasn't cutting anybody down, but I might say something to them about someone on our team like, "This guy's not hitting the ball real well right now" or "He threw a few bad pitches"—little things, no offense intended, but I'd get some sore looks from some of my teammates when I'd say something like that and it came out in the papers.

It wasn't like the whole team was huddled around me in support, to be honest. There were a few other guys—Catfish, Mickey, Kenny Holtzman—who stuck behind me, but there were a lot of guys on the team who were like, "This guy was already out for one year, and now he's out for two years? Why is he still hanging around? Why is George still paying him?" It was the same kind of crap I'd heard the year before. And once again, Thurman would stick up for me a lot when they'd start talking like that.

I remember one day, I was in the clubhouse talking to a couple writers—Joe Gergen and another guy who worked for *Newsday*, one of the Long Island papers. A lot of the guys were out on the field taking batting practice, but I was sitting there in my locker, and they were interviewing me for a piece they were writing. Dick Tidrow and Sparky Lyle came in while we were talking, and Tidrow muttered something derogatory towards me, like, "You need to play a ballgame before you get a write-up!"

I didn't say a word in response, but Thurman heard it. Thurman turned and quietly said to Tidrow, "Get off of him. He's doing the best he can."

After that, they didn't say anything else. That's how it was with Thurman, how much the other players respected him—if Thurman says something, it goes. And he'd stick up for me with the writers, too. Henry Hecht was the only writer who really killed me, and I never understood it. He was a little Jewish guy, and he would just destroy me in the *New York Post* when I was on the DL. He came in to talk to me one day when I was in the clubhouse getting physical therapy, and then the next day I woke up and he'd written something really nasty about me in the paper. And Thurman, when he saw him the next day, really went for his jugular. "How in the world can you do that to him?" he raged at Hecht. "Here's a guy that's on the disabled list because he ran full-speed into a *wall* in spring training. This guy just came back from an operation. This guy gives 120 percent. How in the world can you say that crap about him?" Thurman refused to talk to him after that.

But I soon started seeing other people's stuff shoved into my locker. My name was still up on it, and I still had my own things in there, but I would have to dig through Lou Piniella's extra bats or Don Gullett's extra shoes—or sometimes even our clubhouse guys' cleaning stuff—to get to it. I'd been using the same locker in Yankee Stadium for so many years, some of them really good years, and now suddenly my stuff was buried by the overflow from other people's lockers. It's like you've been working at the same desk in the office for 10 years, and then all of a sudden you get sick, and you come back after six months, and your desk is someone else's desk. I felt like I'd been put out to pasture, like someone had run me out of my home.

The team had lost faith in me, and I knew it. I wanted to get better, and I *was* getting better, but not better enough to play. Sitting there, watching them get dressed, listening to them joke around, with my locker filled with other guys' stuff, I felt like I was being thrown away. That's why I would go into the trainer's room early every day, because it was so embarrassing to be in the locker room. Or I'd be on the training table getting worked on, and then some other guys would come in and they'd have to be worked on, because they were playing that day. They'd be like, "Are you ready to get off? Let someone who's playing today get on there!" It was ripping my heart out.

It was a very lonely time, and I was in a very dark place. I felt like an intruder, like a slug. I'd been a great athlete all my life, but it was all taken away by injuries. I knew I was still a major league ballplayer, but now people were acting like I was ready for the glue factory. But through all of it, Thurman stood behind me. The one good thing about going to the ballpark every day when the team was in town was that I could count on Thurman to come into the trainer's room and talk to me, check in with me, see how I was holding up.

Every single day, he'd ask, "Bloomie, how ya doin'?"

"Oh, I'm coming along," I'd say, but he could see the frustration on my face. Thurman was like my shrink. I could sit down and talk to him about anything. We talked about college football, who was gonna be this year's Heisman candidates; we talked about things that were going on with Tote, we talked about Nat and music, and what shows we were maybe gonna see. And we talked a lot about personal stuff.

Thurman knew what I was going through. My life was gone, and I couldn't get it back. My son, Adam, my little boy, had just been born in '76. That year, when I was injured with my shoulder, my wife, Mara, would bring him to the ballpark for every game that we had. In '77, they did not come to the ballpark. I would just come to the ballpark for rehab, and then basically just go home.

It got to the point where I couldn't sleep good at night. I would wake up in the middle of the night thinking, "Am I ever going to play baseball again? Am I going to play in New York anymore? Do my teammates even care, or are they just dissing me because they look at me as a jinx, a guy that is bad voodoo and they need to stay away from?" They'd always go by me in the clubhouse and say "Hi, Ron," but it's no major conversation.

Thurman, though, he'd always sit with me and talk, never really bringing up baseball, you know, just trying to cheer me up, saying things like, "We can't wait til you get back." Catfish was always great, too. The three of us always clicked, and it was a good feeling.

Thurman really comforted me, like a brother to a brother. It was just the two of us, one-on-one, nobody else around but the trainers, and he would talk to me and make me feel good. I felt bad about confiding in him all the time, and complaining to him about how bad I felt, but he never once acted like it was a burden. He was always there to listen, always encouraging me to keep working, always telling me, "Hang in there! Hang in there!"

As the season went on, I started seeing Thurman on the training table a lot more. He wasn't completely banged up like I was, but his legs were starting to go. Catching is murder on your legs, and this would be his eighth straight season of catching a thousand innings or more, and the workload was definitely taking its toll. In addition to that, he was getting beat up pretty good. During one game against the Orioles, Lee May spiked his hand during a play at the plate, and it got infected so badly that Thurman had to miss a week's worth of games, which drove him absolutely nuts.

Of course, the good part for him was that he could go back and play once the hand healed up. I didn't have that option, because my knee just wasn't there yet. If I'd had access to the medical technology they have now, they could have scoped my knee, and I'd have been back playing again in a couple of months. But they had to cut muscle on muscle, and it was a lot harder to come back from that.

I tried all season to avoid running into George in the hallways, because with him it was always, "Hey, Ron, how are you feeling?" Gabe Paul was the same way, and I didn't want to answer any more questions about my knee. For the most part, I tried to avoid Billy, as well, because on the rare occasions when he would even acknowledge my existence, it would usually be with some nasty remark like, "I've gotta juggle my lineup because of you!" But one day, probably about halfway through the season, I walked into the clubhouse and found Billy sitting there by himself in only his underwear and stirrups. "Hey, Boomer," he said, "come over here and talk to me."

In my mind, I was like, "Uh-oh"—but he seemed in a friendly enough mood, so I followed him into his office and sat down. He said, "How are you doing? Are you pretty close?"

"I don't think so," I replied, which was not what he was expecting to hear; he wanted me to say, "Yeah, I'm pretty close!" Because he wanted me to play. *I* wanted me to play! But I had to be honest with him. And I don't think he ever talked to me again after that.

Another person who was in Billy's doghouse that year was Kenny Holtzman. He was still a very good pitcher, but for some reason or another, Billy would only rarely use him. Kenny told me one day, "I know what you're going through,

Bloomie. A lot of guys I used to play with are going through similar things."

I said, "Yeah, but at least you can still pitch."

"Yeah," he said, "but instead I'm playing crossword puzzles out in the bullpen."

I thought about that for a bit. "Yeah," I said, "and I'm sitting up in the press box, listening to the writers talking smack about the team."

Whenever the team was on the road for a week or 10 days, the Yankees would have a minor league trainer come to the stadium to make sure I got taken care of. Since I wasn't on the road with the team, and I usually wouldn't stay for the whole ballgame when they were playing at home, Thurman and I didn't socialize in '77 as much as we used to. It's not that I didn't want to, but I knew he was concentrating on winning games, and he had a lot different types of personalities on the pitching staff—Catfish, Torrez, Guidry, Gullett, Sparky, Tidrow, Ed Figueroa—to deal with, not to mention the daily craziness with George, Billy, Reggie, or whoever else was throwing a tantrum that week.

But whenever the team had a day off, Thurman would come into the city and meet me, or I would drive to New Jersey where he was living, and we'd have lunch. Sometimes we'd go out to dinner at the Stage Deli after a day game, just like old times. Or we'd go down to Nat's office in Midtown and hang out there, or we'd go up to Nat's place in Purchase and go out to dinner with him, as we had for so many years. Ellie Howard would often join us when we went up to Nat's, but we wouldn't talk about baseball much—which was good, since I felt so miserable about not being able to play. We would just socialize and have fun. It made me feel good to know I had a true friend in Thurman, and that our friendship went deeper than baseball.

This was before Thurman bought his airplane, so during those lunches and dinners, we talked a lot about his real estate holdings. But he was also starting to talk about wanting to be a pilot, so he could fly back to Canton all the time and check in on his properties, as well as see his family more often. Thurman was a business guy, smart as a whip. I mean, if he could keep a team like the Yankees together, he's gotta be a smart guy, right?

Thurman was a very analytical person. Being a good catcher isn't just about getting back there behind the plate and catching and throwing, and he was a very analytical type of catcher. He was also smart enough to sense that I was starting to think about maybe playing somewhere else, once my knee finally healed up.

My contract with the Yankees was going to be up at the end of the season; other than Reggie, Gullett, Catfish, Thurman, and a couple of other people, most of the guys on the team still had one-year contracts. The Yankees never mentioned anything about my contract, because back then they didn't start talking to you about new contracts and salary raises until after the season was over. It didn't even occur to them to think about whether I was gonna leave, because they thought I was going to stay there my whole career. And, after all, I was down in their trainers' room every day, working on my knee.

But Thurman could see the wheels turning in my head. To be honest, I hated to think about leaving New York—these were my people, and they took great, great care of me, even when I was injured. Everywhere I went, I had so many great people to give me a lot of support. When I was on the street down in Manhattan or up in the Bronx, strangers would greet me like an old friend. But when I came to the ballpark, it didn't feel like my home anymore.

Catfish had told me about when he left the A's to go to the Yankees. "It was time for me to leave," he said. He wasn't injured at the time—he was in great shape—but it was time for him to leave because Charlie Finley didn't treat him right. He became a free agent, and George treated him right, and he had a new life in New York. But my life was already in New York. I had it all, if I stayed there. I had the fans, I had my teammates. I knew the writers and the sportscasters. I did speaking engagements. I did bar mitzvahs. I belonged to every synagogue in New York. And then I ran into the wall, and went from the top right down to the bottom.

One day, also about halfway through the season, I sat down with Thurman at Pete Sheehy's gigantic table. It was around noon on the day of an 8:00 game, and nobody else was around, expect for Pete and some of the clubhouse guys. We decided we wanted some food, so I got one of the guys to run out to this deli that was right underneath the El at the Yankee Stadium stop, and get us some corned beef and pastrami.

As we ate our sandwiches, Thurman asked me what was on my mind. "I don't know, Thurm," I told him. "This is the hardest thing in my life, what I've been going through. Maybe I need another home. Because I've been injured for the last two years, maybe I need to go to another team. What do you think?"

"We'd love to have you here, Bloomie," he said, between mouthfuls of pastrami. "I feel like I'd be losing a brother if you left, but I would understand. I see how much you go through, every day, and I know you're doing everything you can possibly do. I haven't been injured like you have—but I can see how, being injured all the time, it's hard to feel like you're part of this. I can see why you might think about going somewhere else. I would understand if you feel you need to make a change."

"What would *you* do?" I asked him. He'd been dropping hints again that he wanted George to trade him to Cleveland, but that always sounded like a bluff to me; I could never picture him in any other uniform.

"Selfishly, I'm gonna say you should stay here," he shrugged. "They love you here, Bloomie. You're so known here, so popular in New York. You've got everything here—

you've got your name on every restaurant menu. You go down to the Garment District, and everybody knows you, everybody wants to shake your hand and give you clothes. You go some other place, and it's a brand-new team, a brand-new city, Everything you've accomplished in New York, you're not gonna be able to take that with you. And what are Nat and I gonna do with you not being here?"

It was nice to hear him say those things, but that really wasn't what I was asking him.

"Yeah," I said, "But you know, be honest with me, now. What would you do?"

He chewed a while before answering.

"Don't even think about it 'til at the end of the year, Bloomie," he finally replied. "See where you are then."

By the end of the season, my knee was about 80 percent better. I still couldn't play on it, but I was back to lifting weights with it, so I knew I was getting close. I also knew that, once the postseason was over, I was going to put my name on the free agency list. I hadn't mentioned it to anybody yet, but I really saw no other option. What if I came back to the Yankees in '78, and then got hurt *again*? What if I broke another bone? I'd have to go out and play with my cast on, or else the guys would all be looking at me like I was jaking.

That October, the Yankees beat the Royals in the playoffs again, and went on to play the Dodgers in the World Series. I didn't even go to any of those games—I just couldn't do it. I had gone to the ALCS and World Series games at Yankee Stadium in '76, and I had great seats—right on the bench. But I felt like I was an overgrown batboy, just sitting there watching the guys play, watching them going out on to the field and coming back. I couldn't do that again this year, especially since I felt more disconnected from the team than ever. I couldn't even bring myself to watch the games on TV or listen to them on the radio, because I knew Phil Rizzuto, Bill White or Frank Messer would probably mention my name on the broadcast, and that would really kill me.

Thurman and I had both signed with the Yankees when they weren't very good, and then we stayed through thick and thin, even as a lot of other ballplayers came and went. We were there when CBS sold the Yankees to George Steinbrenner, and when George started doing everything to make the team great—trading for Nettles and Chambliss and Mickey, bringing in Catfish and Reggie as free agents. But it wasn't easy for us. Playing in New York, everything is magnified a thousand percent; you say one word that is not kosher, and it comes back to you a thousand times. You've gotta be a certain kind of ballplayer to play in that situation. But we both survived New York, and even thrived there.

And now, here we both were, Thurman and I, sitting in the trainers' room before Game 6. The Yankees were on the verge of fulfilling George's dream, the dream of countless Yankee fans who hadn't celebrated a World Series championship in 15 years, and the dream that Thurman and I had been playing for ever since we were kids. Writers from all across the country were swarming around the clubhouse before the game, looking for Thurman, who was comfortably tucked into the quiet sanctuary of the trainers' room. He never liked talking to reporters, especially before a World Series game. None of the writers were looking for me; what would they want to talk to me for? I was all but invisible to them now. In a few hours, Thurman would be exactly where he wanted to be—behind the plate for a World Series game at Yankee Stadium—and I would be back at my apartment in Riverdale.

The Yankees won it all that night, clinching their first world championship in 15 years on the strength of Reggie Jackson's three consecutive home runs. Thurman made some essential contributions, as well, singling in the fourth inning and scoring on Reggie's first homer of the night, and coaxing a complete-game performance out of Mike Torrez. When Torrez caught Lee Lacy's popup for the final out of the Series, Thurman rushed out to hug him, then quickly turned and raced back to the dugout and into the clubhouse before the waves of victory-crazed Yankee fans could overtake him.

It had been another brilliant season for Thurman, who hit .308 with 28 doubles, a career-high five triples, 18 homers, and 100 RBIs. He'd led the Yankees to a 100–62 record and their second straight AL pennant, and now he'd finally earned the World Series ring he'd been working for since the day he signed with the organization in 1968. During the champagne-soaked celebration that followed the historic victory, Thurman got caught up enough in the spirit of the moment to let Bill White briefly interview him for ABC's cameras. "I like to play baseball," he grinned, when Bill asked him if he still wanted to be traded to Cleveland. "I'm gonna play baseball somewhere, I'll tell you that."

I was going to play baseball somewhere, too, but I knew it wasn't going to be in New York City. Nobody realized it that night but me, but Game 6 of the '77 World Series would be the last time I was ever in the Yankee clubhouse as a member of the Yankees.

11

A Fresh Start

It's like some weird dream. I'm back at Yankee Stadium for Opening Day 1978. My boyhood heroes Mickey Mantle and Roger Maris are there, and the sold-out crowd goes crazy as they're driven out onto the field. They present the World Series trophy to New York mayor Ed Koch, who everybody boos. Thurman, Reggie, Mickey, Catfish, Sparky, Gator— everybody's lined up on the field, looking good in their fresh pinstripes, feeling proud as their world championship flag flaps in the April breeze out in center field, and ready to play some baseball. I'm ready to play, too, but I'm standing on the other side of the field from all of them. In a different uniform.

By the end of the '77 season, I was 29 years old, my knee was getting stronger (though it wasn't anywhere near 100 percent), and I knew I still had some gas left in the tank as a player. But I also knew that, after two and a half years in the trainer's room at Yankee Stadium, I needed to go somewhere else.

A lot of people can't play in New York. They can't handle the pressure, the media, the intensity of the fans. But I was one of those guys who *could* play in New York, who *wanted* to play in New York, who loved everything about the place— but I hadn't been able to play in New York the last couple of years, because of all the injuries, and it was affecting how some people saw me, and how I saw myself. I had to make a change, if only for mental purposes. The '77 season felt a re-run of a really bad TV show, and I couldn't bear to watch it again.

So when it came time for players to decide whether they were going to go into the free agent re-entry draft in November, I put my name on the list. I told Thurman, "I'm gonna be a free agent. I'm gonna see if I can play again!"

"You *will* play again, Bloomie" he told me. "There's no doubt in my mind."

When I declared as a free agent, all hell broke loose in the Yankees front office. George called me up and said, "How in the hell can you do this? We stuck by you for three years! We sent you out to L.A. to get your shoulder done, we give you a raise every year. You're part of this team, and with your popularity, you need to be here!"

Gabe Paul called me, Billy called me, even Elston Howard called me, and they were all really angry with me.

George got even angrier when he heard that the Mets wanted to sign me. I had a meeting with Donald Grant and Sheldon Stone, who was my agent at the time. The Mets wanted to give me a four-year deal, but that wasn't solving the problem of leaving the Yankees. I couldn't stay in the same city and go to the Mets. Plus, I didn't want to play at Shea again. I needed a city change.

So I went to Chicago to meet with White Sox owner Bill Veeck. He was an unbelievable man. What a sweetheart he was, and what a character! During my initial meeting with him and Sheldon, he was smoking cigarettes and then stubbing out the butts in an ashtray he'd had built into his wooden leg! I went down to Comiskey Park, and Veeck brought some of the ballplayers in to meet me, like Steve Stone, Wilbur Wood, Eric Soderholm, and Chet Lemon. These guys all lived in Chicago during the off-season, and they all told me what a great town it was, and how much fun the '77 season had been for them in Chicago.

"The South Side Hit Men," as they were fondly dubbed by the local papers, had captured Chicago's imagination in 1977. A motley crew led by "rent-a-stars" Oscar Gamble and Richie Zisk—both of them playing out their options on the way to free agency—bashed a franchise record 192 home runs and spent

most of the summer in first place in the AL West before their pitching and defensive shortcomings finally got the best of them.

It seemed like an endless party at Comiskey that summer, with Sox players taking curtain calls after every home run, broadcaster Harry Caray drunkenly serenading the crowd with "Take Me Out to the Ballgame" during the seventh-inning stretch, and organist Nancy Faust playing the rousing "Na-Na-Na-Na Hey-Hey-Hey Goodbye" chorus of Steam's "Kiss Him Goodbye" whenever the booming Sox bats sent an opposing hurler to the showers. White Sox manager Bob Lemon was a smart baseball man who projected a serene and unflappable air, and the team seemed to radiate a loose and funky harmony that differed sharply from the vibe in the tense, ego-filled Yankees clubhouse. Veeck's charisma and charm, and the appealingly ancient environs of Comiskey Park, also made playing for the White Sox seem like an attractive proposition.

Veeck offered me a guaranteed four-year contract for $650,000. Before I signed my contract, I called Thurman up in Canton, and I said, "Thurman, you're my brother. Here's what they offered me. Before I take it, I'm asking you: What would you do?"

He started laughing and screaming, "Take it! Take it!" But then he asked me, "Do you feel comfortable there? Are you healthy?" Because if I'm not healthy, then I'm taking someone else's money, and he knew I wouldn't feel good about that.

I told him, "Yes, I'm healthy, but I still have some problems with my knee. Hopefully it'll be back to 100 percent by spring."

He said, "Chicago's a great town, and they have a pretty good ball team—they ripped our heads off a few times last year. It's not like New York, Bloomie, but if you feel comfortable there, go for it."

When George found out that I was about to sign with the White Sox, he called me up and offered me the same amount. I thanked him, but I told him that I just couldn't do it. I told him that, with the Yankees, I felt like I was a piece of used property that's been sent to the junkyard, and now I was feeling energized by this new opportunity in Chicago. Plus, I really loved Bill Veeck, so I was like, "I've gotta make the change." I loved George—he was like a second father to me in many ways—and I felt terrible about leaving him, and leaving New York, but I had to go.

In Chicago, I lived at a place called Lake Point Tower, this gorgeous apartment building right on the lake near downtown. There were so many great restaurants in that city, and the people there really welcomed me, especially the Jewish community—once again, I was invited to every bar mitzvah in the city. And on Opening Day at Comiskey, I hit a game-tying home run in the ninth inning off Dick Drago of the Red Sox, and the fans went wild. We won the game, and four days later I hit another long home run to help the team beat the Blue Jays. It seemed like a good omen for my new chapter in Chicago.

Our first road trip of the season included the Yankees' home opener at Yankee Stadium, and I felt such a mixture of emotions being back there. This place had been my home, even though I'd only played one game at the stadium after it was renovated. I went to the ballpark early on Opening Day, before the team bus came to pick us up at the hotel, because I needed some time to take it all in. I had never been to the visiting clubhouse at Yankee Stadium before. Why would I? But now I was walking through the tunnel, going in the opposite direction of where I'd always gone before, and I was seeing a lot of guys underneath the stadium that I knew—stadium workers and reporters. I was hugging some of these guys, because they'd been part of my life for so many years, and it was good to see them again. After getting dressed in the visitor's clubhouse, I decided I had to go into the Yankees clubhouse. Pete Sheehy was in there, of course, and Gene Monahan and Herm Schneider. Guidry was in there, getting ready to take the ball on Opening Day. Piniella and some of the other guys were there. And Thurman was there, too.

He started laughing as soon as he looked up and saw me. "Did you get that from the Salvation Army?" he asked. I was wearing the White Sox uniform with the crazy collar and the leggings—at least I wasn't wearing the shorts like the team had worn a few years earlier, but I have to admit it was still kind of funny looking. I went over and gave him a big hug, and he said, "What would you have done if you had to wear those shorts?"

"That would be pretty ugly with my knee," I laughed. "I'm glad I missed them. Thank god they don't wear those anymore!"

All the guys were laughing. And of course, Billy came by and said, "Make sure you don't run into any walls!" Gee, thanks Billy.

Thurman and I sat there and talked for a while. We talked about our kids, our families, and I told him about my new life in Chicago. Back then, fraternizing with opposing players in the clubhouse was kind of a no-no, but nobody gave us any trouble about it. We were on different teams now, but we were still brothers. He asked me about my shoulder, and I said, "Well, it's okay." It was all the way back, but my knee was still giving me trouble.

His knees were hurting him, too. "My knees are real bad," he said. "My back is hurting. Billy told me that I'm going play more outfield this year." He said they were even thinking about putting him at first base, though they never really did, because they had Chris Chambliss at first. He told me that he'd signed a new deal with the Yankees in spring training; it still wasn't what Reggie was making, which he felt bitter about, but it was big improvement over the previous deal they gave him.

The Yankees swept us in those three games that series, which was painful for me on a whole lot of levels. It was a nice bunch of guys on the White Sox, but it was already clear to me that we weren't a good team. Veeck hadn't been able to afford to sign Oscar Gamble or Richie Zisk to come back for the '78 season, and me and my old pal Bobby Bonds—who had come to the team in a trade with the Angels—were supposed to be their replacements. But neither Bobby or I were hitting very well, our pitching wasn't great, and I could already tell it was going to be a long season. I was starting to think that I'd made a big mistake, and being at Yankee Stadium just intensified that feeling. I ran into George and Gabe Paul on Opening Day, and George wouldn't even say hello. Gabe Paul did, but only to say, "We've got a ring for you. I can't believe you left us!"

Other than seeing Thurman again, the one happy memory I have of that three-game series in New York is the Reggie Bars. On Opening Day, they handed out a Reggie Bar—a new candy bar with Reggie's picture on it—free to every fan who came into the ballpark. Wilbur Wood was pitching for us, and Reggie hit a home run off him, and as soon as the ball went over the fence, everybody threw their Reggie Bars out on the field! They had to stop the game for like 20 minutes while the grounds crew picked up the thousands of candy bars that were all over the field. I was dying laughing, because I knew that Thurman and Billy were going nuts over in the

Yankees dugout, and I could just imagine what Piniella and Nettles and Tidrow and Mickey were saying about it. Reggie, of course, was miffed because he took it to mean that the fans didn't like his candy bar, when really they were just tossing them in the air in celebration. To this day, at Yankees reunions Mickey always says to Reggie, "I'm glad you didn't try to pick up any of those Reggie bars, because you would have dropped those, too!"

Going from New York to Chicago was such a culture shock. It was like driving a station wagon after you've been riding in a Rolls-Royce. The fans were very good to me there, and there was a big Jewish community there. We also had two other Jewish players on the team, Steve Stone and Ross Baumgarten. But we didn't have the Catfish Hunters or Thurman Munsons, the Mickey Rivers or Lou Piniellas, the Chris Chamblisses or Graig Nettleses. We had Chet Lemon and Eric Soderholm, Lamar Johnson, and Claudell Washington—good ballplayers and great guys, but the team chemistry wasn't there.

Playing for Bill Veeck was probably the best thing about the whole experience. Veeck was always having crazy promotions in Chicago. He loved baseball and he was a wonderful man, and I felt very comfortable with him. He was like George a little bit, because he was an outcast among the other owners, and he did what he wanted to do. He just didn't have George's money. But going to Comiskey Park from Yankee Stadium was like night and day. Comiskey Park was a nice old park, but playing there wasn't like playing at Yankee Stadium; it didn't have the same kind of electricity or intensity, especially since we weren't drawing many fans. And putting on the White Sox uniform wasn't at all like putting on the pinstripes. When I put on my Yankees uniform, I felt proud to be part of the team's history. When I put on the White Sox uniform, with the untucked jerseys with the big flaps, it felt like I was getting ready to play for the Ringling Bros. It was a major difference.

You felt the difference on the road, too. With the White Sox, I traveled to all the same cities I went to with the Yankees, but we never had the 500–600 people waiting for autographs when we got off the bus; there might have been one or two. With the Yankees, there were always Yankee fans in other cities who came out to the ballpark to cheer us on. It didn't matter if we weren't doing well, we always had a cheering section wherever we played, and it was a major event when we came to town. People would recognize you at restaurants. "Are you with the Yankees?" You didn't get that with the White Sox— you'd go into restaurants and say you were with the White Sox, and they'd say, "Oh, do you guys have a game tonight?" It was a total downer.

I never really felt like I fit in on the White Sox. I was a little more of a character, more outgoing, than most of the guys on that team. I was used to being in the limelight playing in New York, now I'm playing on a team that's second fiddle to the Chicago Cubs. And that's not to take anything away from my teammates, or from the people of Chicago, but we were the sideshow, not the main event. We weren't Muhammad

Ali, we were the undercard. We weren't Jackie Wilson, we were whatever group they had opening the show for him. It wasn't the worst thing in the world, but for me it was a whole different thing.

Here's a prime example: Bucky Dent. Bucky Dent was with the White Sox for many years, and nobody outside of Chicago had ever heard of him. And then he goes to New York, is on the World Series–winning team in '77, hits that home run off of Mike Torrez and the Red Sox in '78, and now he's BUCKY DENT—he's a superstar. He loved Chicago, but getting traded to the Yankees was the best thing that ever happened to him. Or like Ron Santo—he was a great ballplayer, and totally deserves to be in the Hall of Fame, but if he'd played in New York he would have gotten into the Hall much sooner. That's the kind of difference that playing in New York can make for you, which is why Reggie wanted to be a Yankee.

On July 23, 1978, the Yankees beat the White Sox 3–1, wrapping up a three-game sweep at Comiskey. Thurman played all three games in right field, with Mike Heath catching for the Yankees. Ron pinch-hit for the White Sox in the first game and played first base in the other two. He drove in the only Sox run in the third game, bringing home Eric Soderholm with a two-out single off of Ed Figueroa. In the top of the ninth, Thurman led off the inning by grounding out to third base, and Ron made the putout at first. It was the last time the two friends would play in the same regular-season game.

Thurman and I weren't in contact much during the '78 season. We didn't talk on the phone, but if we had time while I was in New York with the White Sox, or the Yankees came to Chicago to play us, we'd make plans to go out to dinner. But because our teams were in different divisions, we didn't get to see each other as much as we would have if I'd gone to, say, Detroit or Cleveland.

We got together for a meal when the Yankees came to town in July, and spent several nice hours together catching up. Thurman confided in me that he was not having fun in '78 because of all the drama with Billy and Reggie and George. The Yankees had basically the same team as in '77, but there were even more fights in the clubhouse now. Billy was drinking more, and of course the guys didn't want to be around him too much when he was drinking. The drama just kept getting bigger and bigger, and it took away from the team. Every ballpark they went into, the reporters just wanted to talk to the players about the drama, not baseball. All the questions after the ballgame were like, "What do you think of what's happening with Billy and George?" or "What's happening with Billy and Reggie?"

And Thurman's body was breaking down. "I'm constantly having to have therapy for my knees and back," he told me. But he was well aware that, when you're playing in New York, people don't want to see you breaking down—they want to see you perform every night. And if you can't do that, there's drama, big drama. Thurman loved the game of baseball, but he didn't like this drama, didn't like hearing about it every single day.

He brought up the idea of being traded to the Indians. I said, "Thurman, are you sure? I think I made the wrong decision by coming to Chicago, and I would have loved to be a Yankee for life, if things had been different. Don't you want to play out your career in New York?"

But he was really having his doubts. He loved his kids so much, and was so close to Diana and Tote, and he hated to leave them. He was still talking about taking flying lessons and considering buying his own plane so he could spend more time with them. Flying from New York to Canton was no big deal, like only an hour and a half, but Thurman told me George wouldn't allow it. So playing for the Indians seemed the best solution, since Canton was only 45 minutes from Cleveland. "If I can't get the money I want in New York," he said, "I know I can get it in Cleveland, and I won't have to fly home to see my family." They loved him in New York, but he was always a small-town boy at heart.

And Thurman was aggravated. He'd given his all to the New York Yankees, and he just wanted respect. The guys on the team gave him respect, but the front office didn't give him respect. He felt he deserved to be the highest-paid player on the team, other than Catfish. By now, he knew that George would never make good on their verbal agreement, and he was fed up. George used to call downstairs to the clubhouse and try to talk to Thurman on the phone, and Thurman wouldn't talk to him. So he'd send guys down from the front office to tell Thurman, "George really wants to talk to you."

To which Thurman would say, "Go fuck yourselves. I don't want to talk to him! If he wants to talk to me, he can come down here." But that was him. And as angry as he was at George, he never let his contract situation bother him on the field. After the ballgame, he might be stewing, but he would play hard in every single game. He just wanted his share. But like always, he never took it out on the field, never broke a bat on the field or kicked the bag, never made a fool out of himself in public. Because he was a leader.

Thurman was a smart guy. He knew he was getting older and more bashed-up, and he was starting to look ahead to his life after baseball. He told me that when his career ended, he wasn't going to stay in the game; he didn't want to be a coach or a manager. He loved being a player—but when he couldn't play any longer, he wanted to focus on business. And that's why he bought so much property in Canton. He asked me if I'd thought at all about what I was going to do when my playing days were over. I confessed that I hadn't. Even though my knee was still only at about 75–80 percent, and I had to put ice on my shoulder for several hours before every game, I figured I still had a few more years to think about it. "Don't wait, Bloomie," he cautioned me. "You need to start thinking about this now."

The day after the Yankees left town, it came out in the papers that Billy got drunk at O'Hare while the team was waiting for their flight, and had insulted George and Reggie to a bunch of reporters. George gave Billy the choice of resigning or being fired, and Billy resigned. And then George hired Bob Lemon, who Veeck had fired just a few weeks earlier. Veeck brought Larry Doby in to replace him, and I'm sorry to say it but he was just the worst. We didn't have a good team, but we did even worse with Larry than we did with Bob.

The White Sox finished the 1978 season in fifth place in the AL West, their 71–90 record (almost a complete reversal from the '77 squad's 90–72 mark) putting them 20.5 games behind the division champion Kansas City Royals. Ron played in 61 games that season for the White Sox, mostly as a DH, and hit .231 with five home runs and 22 RBIs in 169 plate appearances. Thurman's power numbers dropped significantly in 1978—he hit only six homers—and this was the first season since 1974 where he didn't drive in 100 runs or more, but he still hit a solid .297 and led the Yankees to their third straight AL East flag. He also caught 125 games, despite his aching knees and back.

For Thurman and his teammates, winning the AL East was even sweeter this time. Unlike in 1976 and 1977, where the Yankees had spent the majority of the year in first place, the Yankees had battled back from a 14-game deficit in mid-July to force a one-game playoff with the hated Boston Red Sox. Two batters after Bucky Dent hit his famous home run to put the Yankees up 3–2 in the top of the seventh, Thurman doubled home Mickey Rivers to make it 4–2, a crucial insurance run on the way to the Yankees' eventual division-clinching 5–4 victory. In the team's four-game ALCS defeat of the Royals, Thurman hit .278, complete with a game-winning two-run homer off Doug Bird in the bottom of the eighth inning of Game 3. And he went 8-for-25 with three doubles, seven RBIs, and five runs scored as the Yankees beat the Dodgers four games to two for their second straight world championship. Thurman—who earlier that day had been the subject of a nasty but grudgingly appreciative character study by L.A. Times *columnist Jim Murray that referred to him as, among other things, "Thurman Monster"—caught the last out of the World Series, a pop-up off the bat of Ron "the Penguin" Cey, and the team celebrated on the Dodger Stadium mound.*

It was a rough season for me in Chicago. Even though my knee was doing better, I still couldn't put enough weight on my left leg to really swing the bat the way I wanted to, and I had to adjust my swing because of it. And once you start adjusting things you've been doing your whole life, things get difficult. I wanted to do well for the White Sox, and especially for Bill Veeck, but the press was already starting to call me a "free agent bust," which didn't make me feel too good. I hoped that things would be better in '79.

I watched some of the Yankees' games in the postseason that year. I was proud of Thurman, as always, and I was glad to see them win. It hurt maybe a little less to watch them play in the World Series than it had in '76 and '77, because at least I was playing ball again, but it still hurt. In my heart, that Yankees team was still my team, only now I was watching them in Chicago. I called Thurman to congratulate him when he got back to Canton, but all he really wanted to talk about was how happy he was to be home with Diana and the kids. He was happy to have won the World Series, but it had been a hard season and now he just wanted to watch college football and not think about baseball for a while. We talked about maybe getting together over the winter, either him coming up to Chicago or my family going down to see him and Diana and the kids, but we never got around to making it happen. That was okay, though; we knew we were friends for life, and we'd have plenty of time to hang out together in the future.

12

Like a Bad Dream

The last time I ever saw Thurman was in March 1979, at spring training. The Yankees came to Sarasota to play an exhibition game against us, and we went to Fort Lauderdale a few days later to play them. Thurman played in both games; I didn't play in either of them.

We sat down and talked about our winters. He'd taken up flying like he'd talked about during the summer. He'd finally cleared it with George, and he'd even bought himself a plane. Right off the bat, I thought this was a bad idea. I loved Thurman like a brother and I trusted him, but you couldn't have paid me any amount of money to go up with him in a small plane. Knowing Thurman as I did, it was too easy for me to picture him saying, "Watch me do this! Watch me do that! Somebody told me I couldn't do this, so I'm going to do it!" There was a devilish side to him, and I sure didn't want to see it come out when he was in the cockpit. Not that I would have gone up in a small plane with anyone else either, but I thought of Thurman as a brother and a teammate, not a pilot.

He asked me how I was doing, and I said, "I'm slowing down. I'm getting injections in my knees and shoulder. I think I'm breaking apart now. I'm hitting the ball sometimes, but I'm really not playing up to my expectations." I'd been working out all winter, but I was still struggling at the plate. "If I make it to the end of this season," I told him, "I'll be really lucky."

He nodded. "Whatever you do, Bloomie, I'm with you, I'm for you." He said that his knees and back were getting more beat up. He told me to keep in contact with him, whatever happens, and let him know what's going on. He gave me a goodbye hug after the second game and told me, "I'll see you during the season!" but it never got that far. I was released by the White Sox the next day.

I'd had a fairly good spring with the White Sox, but I was hurting. My shoulder was bad, my knee was bad, and I could only run the bases at maybe half the speed I used to. Things were clearly going downhill. Just how downhill became clear one day when I was taking BP before a game in Sarasota, and all of a sudden Bill Veeck walked out on the field. He was hopping around on his wooden leg, saying hello to everybody. Lamar Johnson was over at first base fielding grounders, and he's talking to Lamar while I'm taking some swings. All of a sudden, I hit a line drive to first, and Bill stuck his wooden leg out to stop it—the ball hit his leg and just dropped to the ground. Back in the day, when I was hitting the ball really hard, a line drive off my bat would have taken his wooden leg right off. But this time, the ball hit his leg and just plopped softly into the dirt, right in front of him. People were dying laughing, and that's the moment I knew that I was going to be released. I knew I was done. Sure enough, Bill and Roland Hemond took me into the office soon afterward and they gave me my release. I really couldn't blame them; I would have released me, too.

I got contacted by the Angels, the Pirates, and maybe three or four others, but I knew there wasn't any point in calling them back; I just didn't want to go through that anymore.

Thurman called me when he heard I'd gotten released. He said, "I'm sorry to hear about it. Is there anything I can do for you?"

"No, Thurm," I said, "there's really nothing you can do. But thank you."

My career was over with; it had just died. But my relationship with Thurman never died. Nobody thought I'd ever come back from hitting that wall in Winter Haven, no one except Thurman. He told me that I should be proud of myself for working as hard as I did, that maybe I didn't do as well with the White Sox as I'd hoped, but that it was a serious accomplishment that I'd made it back to baseball at all, given my injuries. I knew he was right, but for the moment I just wanted to crawl into a hole and hide from the world.

Thurman always told me, "You need to prepare for when your career is over." He always had one eye on his family's financial future, even before I knew him. When I was with the White Sox, Steve Stone told me that Thurman had been very frugal with his money even back when they played together at Kent State. And Thurman was always talking about business and real estate. Whenever we'd meet up for breakfast on the road, he'd be reading *The Wall Street Journal* and the stock market pages of the newspaper. He really enjoyed it, but he was also really smart about it.

But I never thought my career was going to end, or at least that it wouldn't end this soon, because we lived in a dreamworld when we were playing in New York. Especially me, because everywhere I went, Jewish people from cab drivers to presidents of banks would stop to tell me how proud they were of me. I was on the cover of *Sports Illustrated* and *The Sporting News*, I had a sandwich named after me at the Stage Deli, I had an endless supply of free suits from the Garment District, and of course, Nat could get me anything I asked for. It was an amazing existence, but it wasn't reality, and reality hit me hard.

I wasn't into business like Thurman. Thurman had a game plan, and unfortunately I really didn't. My life was baseball, my life was athletics. Of course, I could have returned to New York. Nat called me and told me, "Move back to New York and do TV!"

I said, "No, I've gotta go back to Atlanta and take care of my mom and dad."

It was very hard for me to be in New York City now, because I knew people would recognize me. When I was playing, I loved that, but now it would be like, "What are you doing?"

"Nothing."

Every time I'd talk to him on the phone, Thurman kept on saying, "Don't feel that way, Bloomie! Everybody's gotta go through this."

And I said, "Yeah, but not at 30 years old. I'm supposed to have 10 more good years, and the last two and a half years I've been on the disabled list." It was like a career divorce for me.

I wanted to run away. I didn't want to talk to anybody. But I would continue to call up Thurman every week or two, when I knew he was in one city or another, and I knew what hotels the Yankees were staying at. He was flying home a lot at that point, so sometimes I'd call him in Canton. He'd always ask me how I was doing and tell me what him and Nat were up to. "We talk about you all the time," he said. "You should fly up to New York and go out to lunch with us like we used to. I'm sure Nat can put you up at his place!"

Nat kept asking me to come up, too, to hang out with him and Thurman and the gang. Part of me wanted to go, but part of me was worried that I wouldn't fit in with them anymore, now that I wasn't a ballplayer and didn't really have anything going on in my life. I did go to New York that summer to do some engagements, but I didn't go back to Yankee Stadium or to see Nat—I just couldn't. Thurman and I were supposed to go to lunch two or three times while I was up there, but things came up and it didn't happen.

After you've been released from a team, it feels like your whole body has transformed... you feel like you're not part of anything. You've been doing something since you were practically a baby, and you were drafted No. 1 by the Yankees, and you've been on some great teams with some great players, and then you go to the White Sox, which isn't a great team but you're still playing in the major leagues for a legendary owner, and then all of a sudden you get released and your career is over. You never think about this moment when you're playing.

It was very difficult. Anyone who knows me knows what an upbeat guy I am, but I went through a serious depression, where it was very hard to go out of the house. It was very hard to talk to people and answer questions like, "What does it feel like to not play baseball anymore?" You wake up every single day and you're at home; there's no ballpark to go to, no road trips to prepare for. I told Thurman all of this stuff during our phone calls, and he was very sympathetic. He would tell me to keep my head up, and then he would say something to try and get me to laugh. And usually, that would make me feel a little better.

I last spoke to Thurman about two weeks before his plane crash. The Yankees had just come back from a road trip, and I was in Atlanta. Thurman was feeling a little more beaten down than usual; in addition to his knees and his back, his arm was sore and his hands were starting to give him trouble.

He'd been taking foul balls off his throwing hand and spikes to his glove hand for years, and if you looked at his knuckles they were all mashed up. When Thurman first came up to the majors, he wouldn't use a batting glove while hitting, but during his last few years, when he started getting beat up, he started using batting gloves and a lot of pine tar to grip the bat, so I knew his hands were bothering him. The pain didn't bother him enough that he couldn't play—he'd caught over 80 percent of the team's games so far in 1979—but he was hurting constantly, and Billy was talking again about moving him to first base or the outfield to give him a break.

Nineteen seventy-nine was a tough year for the Yankees. George had brought Billy back to replace Bob Lemon, who had lost the will to manage after his son died in a car crash. Thurman said they were playing better under Billy than they had under Lem, and that it was really nice to have Bobby Murcer back on the team (the Yankees had traded a minor leaguer to the Cubs for him in June), but they were still stuck in fourth place in the division, a good 10 games or so in back of the Orioles. Scotty McGregor was pitching really well for the O's at the time, and Thurman and I talked about that, because he'd been in the Yankees organization for several years before they traded him to Baltimore in '76.

Scotty never pitched a regular-season game for the Yankees, but Thurman worked with him every spring training from '73 to '76. Scotty was a pitcher like Whitey Ford or Tom Glavine; he didn't have a great fastball, but he had good movement.

When he first came to camp, he was throwing everything straight over the plate, but Thurman took him on as a project and taught him how to work the corners. Thurman always had that touch, that ability to take a pitcher to another level. Even when I run into Scotty today, he'll tell me, "Thurman made me the pitcher I was."

Because he was Thurman's pet project, and because I hung out with Thurman all the time, Scotty and I became close, as well. In '75, Scotty and I roomed together during spring training, because Thurman had Diana and their kids down there with him. Shortly after they went back to Canton, we had to go to San Juan, Puerto Rico, to play the Pirates in an exhibition series; a new youth sports complex was being built there in Roberto Clemente's honor, and the two-game series was raising money for the building fund. Thurman stayed with me and Scotty the night before we went, because we had to catch the plane to San Juan the first thing in the morning.

We probably should have called it an early night, but instead Thurman, Scotty, Bobby Bonds, and myself went out to Pete & Lenny's, a nightclub on Commercial Boulevard, to listen to music. I was never a drinker, but this barmaid took a liking to us, and the guys told me that they'd give me 10 or 15 bucks if I would get drunk. Usually, I'd order one vodka gimlet and nurse it until all the ice melted. But they got this girl to bring me a fifth of Southern Comfort, and I drank the whole thing out of the bottle. It did nothing to me, so they had her bring me a second bottle, and I drank all of that one, too. And I swear, I got so sick.

My head was spinning and I was trying to walk, but I couldn't. Thurman and Bobby and Scotty held me up and walked me out of the place, got me into a car, and got me back to the hotel. Thurman threw me into the swimming pool, and then they all pulled me out and took me up to my room.

I woke up like four hours later, and I was sick as a dog, I couldn't get up. My head was spinning, and I was still in the same wet clothes. I was dying. I was more than dying! Scotty and Thurman dragged me to the ballpark, where the bus was waiting to take us to the airport for our flight. But when we got there, I realized I didn't have shoes on. Everyone was all nicely dressed in their sports jackets, and I had nothing—I was still wearing the same clothes from the night before, and I was barefoot. Bill Virdon looked at me but didn't say a word. We got on the bus at the ballpark and went to the Fort Lauderdale airport, got on the plane, and I got in my seat and tried to go to sleep. Rizzuto said hello to me as he passed me in the aisle. I just looked up at him and said, "Please kill me."

I realized that I'd also forgotten to pack any clothes or toiletries. I had my uniform and equipment packed, because the team had packed those for us. My clothes were not wet anymore, but they were stuck to me, and I smelled like a sea cow. We got to Puerto Rico and checked into our hotel, and I passed out in the bed as soon as I got to my room.

When we went to the ballpark that night, I found out that Bill Virdon had penciled me into the starting lineup. I was so sick, I was throwing up. I was dying out there. Virdon put me out in right field, and I couldn't even stand up straight. I struck out four times at the plate. I was still sick the next day, and they made me play the next game, and I struck out four more times and made a couple of errors. I wound up being sick for the whole week. I couldn't eat, I couldn't drink anything, I was a dead guy walking. To this day, I can't even get close to liquor.

And that's what Thurman and I talked about during our last phone call. "Bloomie, remember how sick you got out there?" he ragged me.

"Oh yeah, I remember," I said. "You got me drunk, threw me in a pool, didn't take care of me on the road, and watched me die in front of 15,000 fans. What a great team captain you were!" And we both laughed hysterically.

On the afternoon of August 2, 1979, Thurman crashed his new Cessna Citation I/SP jet while taking a practice spin at Akron-Canton Regional Airport. His two passengers, flight instructor Dave Hall and Thurman's new real estate partner Jerry Anderson, survived, but they were unable to extract Thurman from the wreckage before it went up in flames.

His funeral service was held four days later in Canton, with the entire Yankees team in attendance. Bobby Murcer gave the eulogy, quoting poet and philosopher Angelo Patri: "The life of a soul on Earth lasts longer than his departure. He lives on in your life and the life of all others who knew him."

I was at home in Atlanta when I heard the news about the crash. I was watching TV, and somebody called me up—I think it was Marty Appel—and asked me, "Did you hear?"

"Did I hear what?"

"Thurman got killed in a plane crash."

"No, he didn't," was all I could say. It was like my own life was taken out of me, like a ghost came into my stomach, took my heart out and left. It stunned me so much; I felt completely empty. I know how exactly how Bobby and Piniella and Nettles and Billy and all the other players and coaches felt that day. It was so hard to even begin to process what had happened. It all felt like a bad dream.

I didn't go to his funeral. I tried everything I could to get a flight to Canton, but I was so numb, and it was tough to figure out travel arrangements in my state of mind. There were no direct flights to Canton, and all the flights to Cleveland were full... and in the end, I didn't go, which I really regret now. I couldn't sleep the night before his funeral; I just tossed and turned thinking about him, remembering all the time we'd spent together, and wondering what his last minutes had been like. They showed the funeral on TV the next day, and

I couldn't even watch it; it just tore me up too much. It was hard for me to even believe that it had happened. Even to this day, I can't believe that he left us so early, and in such an awful way. I just hope he didn't suffer too much. I can't think about that; it just tears my heart out.

Much later, I read about the investigations they'd done into the crash, and some interviews with the guys who had been with him on that flight. And it occurred to me: Thurman was a leader, a captain, literally up until he took his last breath. When his plane crashed, the first thing he did was ask the two guys who went with him if they were okay, and then he ordered them to leave the airplane and get to safety, because he knew they wouldn't be able to free him from the cockpit in time. Those guys were his teammates up in the air, and his first thought was to make sure his teammates were all right. That's definitely the Thurman I knew.

Epilogue

What Might Have Been

Neither Thurman or I got to play ball for anywhere near as long as either of us hoped we would. But we were lucky enough to do something that we loved for a living. I was pretty good at it. Thurman, of course, was great at it.

We packed so much into the relatively short time we played together, and we played together through such a crucial period—not just in Yankees history, where the foundation was laid for the championship teams of the late 1970s, but also in baseball history. We played together through years that included a strike, a lockout, the introduction of the DH, the introduction of free agency, and the expansion of the American League. We played alongside and against some of the greatest players to ever take the field, in some of the greatest ballparks ever built, and we had a great time doing it.

People always ask me how I think the rest of Thurman's career would have played out if he hadn't died in the plane crash. Personally, I think he had at least three or four more good seasons left in him. He was hitting .302 just over a week before he died, and though he didn't put up much in the way of power numbers in '79, I think the wear and tear of catching had a lot to do with that. If Thurman could have been talked out from behind the plate to actually play most of his games at first base, in the outfield or as a DH, I believe at least some of that old pop would have returned to his bat.

Would Thurman have remained a Yankee? During his last couple of seasons, he talked all the time about how he wanted to be traded to Cleveland so he could be closer to his family. But as much as Thurman loved Diana and their kids—and he was absolutely head-over-heels for them—I just can't picture him in an Indians uniform, or in any uniform other than that of the New York Yankees. Saying "I want to be traded to Cleveland" was Thurman's way of blowing off steam, of giving the finger to George Steinbrenner when he didn't feel like George was treating him right. If Thurman had lived, I think George would have given him a big contract just to put that uniform on and be the Yankee captain in 1980 and beyond, even if he was only playing in 100 games a year. That's the kind of owner George was; if you played hard for him— and no one played harder than Thurman—he rewarded you, he considered you part of his family, and he'd do anything in the world for you. Plus, there's nothing like putting on those pinstripes and playing in New York City, and I think down deep Thurman knew it. Unlike me, he wouldn't have had to go play somewhere else before he figured that out.

Besides, even though he and George used to fight all the time, George loved Thurman. They were two tough guys from Ohio, and neither of them would back down from anyone. They used to get right in each other's faces and really yell. Thurman would say to George, "Eff you!" But that just made George love him more. George didn't like anybody that was weak; he wanted you to fight back. If you fought back, he'd have your back. And if you didn't fight back, he'd start thinking about getting rid of you. And I can't imagine him ever wanting to get rid of Thurman. Also, all the drama surrounding Reggie and Thurman—which had driven Thurman crazy in '77 and '78—had largely calmed down by '79. I don't know that they ever would have become the best of friends, but after winning two world championships together, they'd finally established a respectful relationship, giving Thurman one less reason to want to leave New York.

Would Thurman have become a manager after he retired? To be honest, I don't think so. He definitely had the brain for it, but he often said to me, "The only way I'd want to stay in baseball is as the owner of a team." He loved the game, and he loved motivating players and being a leader, but I don't think he would have liked filling out the lineup card every day. And I *know* he would have hated having to talk to the press after the game. He would have fought and feuded with all the writers. Billy Martin had his problems with the writers, but he liked to talk, and he knew what to say to them. But I can still see Thurman throwing a bottle at Dick Young one time because Dick wrote something bad about him in the paper. Him and the writers did not get along, and I can't imagine his attitude towards them would have changed just because he'd become a manager. If anything, it would have probably gotten worse!

The more I think about how baseball has changed since our playing days, the less I think that Thurman could have managed now. When he was catching, every starting pitcher went out to the mound looking to pitch at least seven innings. Thurman would always pace his pitchers, because he wanted them to be able to go the distance, and he'd call the game knowing that the pitcher would be going through the opposing lineup three times—especially a guy like Catfish, who would get better as the game went on. And then you'd have your stopper who could come in for an inning or two if you needed him—and who could actually pitch for two or even three innings per appearance. Thurman would have been so turned off by the idea of a starting pitcher only having to go five innings and then being replaced by an endless parade of relievers. That would have driven him completely nuts.

Our teammate Lou Piniella wanted to get back in the game as a manager, and he turned out to be a really good one, which didn't surprise me at all. But like I said, Thurman was more interested in reading *The Wall Street Journal* than he was in reading the sports pages. And being who he was, Thurman had a lot of investment opportunities in Canton—especially after he started making some real money—and he would always talk about buying commercial property, buying shopping centers, things like that. Once he made enough money to do it, I could see him going in with a group and buying a team, like Derek Jeter did with the Marlins. Maybe he would have gone in on a buyout of the Indians. I can definitely see him as an owner-type figure, though he wouldn't have micromanaged everything like George did.

It's also possible that, when Thurman retired from playing, George would have offered him a front office position with the Yankees, maybe even in a GM role like Stick Michael or Brian Cashman. It's hard to picture Thurman working directly under George, though. They would have fought all the time with each other—and again, Thurman would have hated having to talk to the press about whatever deal he'd just pulled off.

Another question people ask me all the time is, "Why isn't Thurman in the Hall of Fame?" It's a good question. I truly believe Thurman *should* be in the Hall of Fame, and it's not just because he was my teammate and my friend. In my view, his skills, his accomplishments, his leadership, and what he did for the game of baseball—and, especially, for the New York Yankees—qualify him for a place in the Hall.

While it's true that his career wasn't as long as it should have been, what a career it was! From '70 to '79, he was an All-Star catcher seven times, a three-time Gold Glove winner, the AL Rookie of the Year in '70, and the AL MVP in '76. When he came up with the Yankees at the end of '69, it was not a great team—but by '76, he was leading the Yankees to their first World Series in 12 years, and then to two straight World Series championships, and he played brilliantly in all three.

Would the Yankees have gone to the World Series three years in a row without Thurman? I don't think so. There was not a more important player on those teams than Thurman, especially in '77 and '78 when he really kept them together. Leadership is not something that shows up in the box scores or the statistics, but every guy on those '77 and '78 championship teams could tell you how crucial Thurman's leadership skills were to maintaining a winning attitude on the field even while all the Bronx Zoo chaos was swirling around them. Do they take that sort of thing into consideration at the Hall of Fame? They should—because it was just unbelievable what he meant to that team. And he was the greatest catcher I ever saw.

Unfortunately, Thurman wasn't the greatest guy in the world when it came to the writers, and I think that hurt him in the end. It took a lot away from his Hall of Fame candidacy, because a lot of writers still look at him as a bully to this day. He alienated a lot of writers, and he got a bad rap for it. If he'd been friendlier and more talkative with the writers, I think it would have definitely helped his case, but that just wasn't Thurman—and Thurman was never going to pretend to be something that he wasn't, even if it would have made his life easier.

I didn't expect Thurman to get in on the first ballot, but I was shocked and saddened to learn that he never got more than 15.5 percent of the vote. Because if the Hall of Fame voting was by the fans, he would have been in there long ago. In New York, if you don't run out a ball, or if you take yourself out of the lineup because you don't feel up to playing, it's magnified 1,000 percent; the fans will never forget about it or forgive you for it. And Yankee fans know Thurman never, ever jaked, and that he always showed up to play even when he was hurting. This was a guy who spent a decade as the Yankees' starting catcher, played hard every time he went out there, and got banged up a lot as a result, and yet he never once went on the DL. If Thurman was feeling good, bad, whatever, he was always ready to get out there and get dirty and call a great game.

The Yankees had some really good teams in '80 and '81, the years immediately after his death, but they couldn't quite get back to the mountaintop. They lost to the Royals in the playoffs in '80, then lost to the Dodgers in the '81 World Series. But if Thurman hadn't been killed in the plane crash and had stayed with the team, he might have made the difference in both series. And if he'd led them to another couple of World Series as their captain, and won another ring or two in the process, I think there would be no question at all of him getting into the Hall.

To me, it comes down to this: The Yankees are the premier franchise in baseball history, and you've got a guy who meant so much to that franchise during a 10-year period, a decade where they went from mediocrity to winning three consecutive AL pennants and two straight World Series championships. If this guy is that important to this important team, how does that not translate into a place in the Hall of Fame?

As Yankees, Thurman and I had three different "home" ballparks: We started together at the true Yankee Stadium, the old "House That Ruth Built," and then we had to go play at Shea Stadium for a couple of years, and then we came back to the rebuilt Yankee Stadium. And now there's a new Yankee Stadium, located 300 yards away from the site of the old one, built on Macombs Dam Park, where we had to practice during the strike in '72. It's a new stadium, but in many ways it's still the same as when we were teammates—it's still right in the middle of the Bronx, you've still got the subways right there, you've still got the Grand Concourse and all the stores on 161st Street and River Avenue.

The new stadium is like a baseball park with a museum in it, but the old Yankee Stadium was like a museum to us. It was our museum, a place filled with so much amazing history.

Even to this day, people will come to New York City and take a tour of Yankee Stadium, just like they go to the Empire State Building or Ellis Island. Tour buses are always stopping in front of it, and tourists get out to take pictures of it. It's not even the old Yankee Stadium, the one we played in, but it doesn't matter. It's still *Yankee Stadium*. It's still sacred ground.

Whenever I go back there, for Old-Timers' Day or if I'm in town for any other reason, it's like the old times all over again. I'll walk through the tunnels of the new stadium, and I'll see stuff from the old stadium that they brought over to the new one, and all of a sudden it's like I'm in *The Twilight Zone*; it's like I've gone into a time machine that's taking me back 40, 45, 50 years. I'll see photos on the walls, and I'll instantly remember when and where they were taken, and I'll remember the people in them and what we were talking about at that moment. I'll remember certain games, certain plays, certain moments, and I'll look out at the field and see Thurman taking his hacks out in the batting cage or putting on his orange chest protector and shin guards in the dugout and getting ready to go out and catch the game.

They have Thurman's locker there in the museum at Yankee Stadium, with his uniform and his bat and his glove in it, and it looks just like it did when he was playing. The glove still has pine tar on it, just like it did when he was three lockers away from me, when we would talk back and forth, joking around and giving each other a hard time, listening to music and figuring out where we were going to go eat after the game.

Every team that comes in to play the Yankees, they all want to go out and see the monuments at Yankee Stadium, see the names and the history. There's only one team that has that, and that's the Yankees. I'll go down to Monument Park and stand there looking at Thurman's plaque. Whenever I do that, it always feels like he's looking down at me, and I can picture him hugging me and talking to me. I'm reminiscing, thinking about us hanging at the Roxy or the Stage, eating pastrami sandwiches and matzah ball soup, thinking of us sitting around and shooting the bull with Nat and his guys. I don't think about the plane crash or the bad times when I'm out there. I just think about the good times.

Over 40 years later, it's still hard for me to believe that Thurman's gone, and that he left us the way he did. But I will always remember the good times, and all the things we did together in those days when we were joined at the hip. I was very lucky to know him, to play on the same team with him, and to have that friendship with him. Thurman was my teammate, but he was my brother as well. I loved him an awful lot, and he's still in my heart. He always will be.

Acknowledgments

From Ron:

In writing this book, I am indebted to my wonderful family—my wife, Beth; my son, Adam, and his wife, Adrianne; my grandchildren, Mila and Gabe Blomberg; and my daughter, Chesley, and her husband, Austin Epps. To Mara Young, for being a great mother to our son and for all she brings to this family. Also to my lifelong friend and cohort in crime, Sheldon (STON-AH) Stone; to Lenny Kosberg for his profound counsel, coaching, and commitment; and to Allison Kosberg and Joe Garrido.

From Dan:

First, I'd like to thank my friend and fellow author David Jordan, who called me one day in early 2019 to tell me that Ron Blomberg was looking for a writer to collaborate on a book project. Big thanks are also due to our agent, Rob Wilson, whose belief and diligence were crucial in finding a home for this book; to Kyle Wagner of the *New York Daily News*, who helped shed much-needed light on our project-in-progress by commissioning Ron and me to write a remembrance piece on the 40th anniversary of Thurman's passing; to Diana Munson, whose generosity, kindness, and support have meant the world to us; and to Jesse Jordan, our extremely patient and understanding editor at Triumph Books.

I'd also like to thank all of those who (whether they were aware of it or not) helped keep this project rolling along the way with their ideas, enthusiasm, assistance, personal memories, and/or writerly moral support: most notably Marty Appel, Joe Bonomo, the late, great Terry Cannon, Bill Crandall, Jason Dummeldinger, Michael Grossbardt, Charlie Hunter, Yusuf Lamont (Herman Munster R.I.P.), Rob Neyer, Fritz Peterson, Mike Randle, James Rotondi, Bill Sablesak, Adrienne Statfeld, Jason Turbow, Darren Viola, and Josh Wilker. And, of course, my family—especially my wife, Katie; my parents, Lyn Delliquadri, Irwin Epstein, and Fran Yancovitz; and my sister, Rebecca Epstein—whose love and support helped me endure the weirdness and awfulness of 2020. Most of all, I'd like to thank Ron for being such a lovely person and such an absolute pleasure to work with, and Thurman Munson for being one of the players who turned me on to the great game of baseball in the first place. Thurman has already long been enshrined in my personal Hall of Fame, but my fondest wish is that this book will help move the needle a little further in terms of him finally being inducted into the Hall of Fame in Cooperstown.

About the authors

RON BLOMBERG spent eight seasons in the majors with the New York Yankees and the Chicago White Sox, and was twice voted "Most Popular Person in New York" during his playing days with the Yankees. He earned a place in Cooperstown, thanks to becoming the first designated hitter to make a plate appearance in an official MLB game (he walked with the bases loaded), and he was inducted into the National Jewish Sports Hall of Fame in 2004. He is the author of *Designated Hebrew: The Ron Blomberg Story*.

DAN EPSTEIN is the author of the 1970s baseball histories *Big Hair and Plastic Grass: Baseball and America in the Swinging '70s* and *Stars and Strikes: Baseball and America in the Bicentennial Summer of 1976*. He writes about baseball, music, and pop culture for a variety of outlets, including *Rolling Stone*, *Revolver*, and the *Jewish Daily Forward*. He lives in Greensboro, North Carolina.